C000076239

"What the author does so well is to group sights
in a logical geographical order and then figure out
the quickest or most interesting way of getting
from one place to another. Often these transitions
are as interesting as the destinations."
— **Cape Cod Times**

About **London for the Independent Traveler:**

"...for travelers who don't have time to plan and don't want to go on a
group tour who want hints on seeing the city's famous sites
as well as some fascinating places that aren't well known."
— **Associated Press**

"...a new approach to seeing this great and venerable city."
— **Footloose Librarian**

"Full of wonderful information for seeing the most of London
you can see in three days, whether it's your first or tenth trip.
For me, the real charm of this guide is its practicality."
— **Minnesota Reviews**

New York for the Independent Traveler was awarded the title
of **Best Travel Guide** in 1989 by the Publishers Marketing Association.
Now this award-winning guidebook is updated, revised, enlarged
and even better!

New York for the Independent Traveler was selected by the
United States Information Services for the **Travel America Book** Exhibit,
representing the best in U.S. Publishing. It was shown
in 75 countries throughout the world.

Other books by Ruth Humleker

LONDON FOR THE
INDEPENDENT TRAVELER

(Revised and Updated Edition)

NEW YORK

FOR THE INDEPENDENT TRAVELER

*Fun self-guided
tours with
special maps,
step-by-step
itineraries
and floor plans*

RUTH HUMLEKER

Marlor Press, Inc.
Saint Paul, Minnesota

NEW YORK FOR THE
INDEPENDENT TRAVELER

(Revised and Updated Edition)

A Marlin Bree Book
Published by Marlor Press, Inc.
Copyright 1997 by Ruth Humleker
Maps by Dick Humleker
Mary Strasma, Assistant Editor

ISBN 0-943400-93-7
Printed in the United States of America
Third Edition
Distributed to the book trade by Contemporary Books, Chicago

Disclaimer: Prices, facilities and services are subject to change at any time. The author and the publisher have made best efforts prior to publication to secure current data. Readers should check prices, facilities and services to meet their own needs. Not responsible for errors and ommissions. This book is only intended as a general guide to various sights and attractions; travelers should use their own judgment and discretion on specific events, times, and places. In any event, Marlor Press Inc, and the author, are not responsible for price changes, schedules, services, availabilities, facilities, agreements, damages, or loss or injury of any kind.

Library of Congress Cataloging-in-Publication Data

Humleker, Ruth.
New York for the independent traveler : fun self-guided tours with special maps, step-by-step itineraries and floor plans / Ruth Humleker ; (maps by Dick Humleker ; illustrations by Marlin Bree). -- Rev. and updated ed., 3rd ed.
p.   cm.
Includes Index
ISBN 0-943400-93-7 (pb)
1. New York (N.Y.) -- Tours. 2. Manhattan (New York, N.Y.) -- Tours. 3. Walking - New York (State) -- New York --Guidebooks. I. title.
F128. 18. H86   1997
917.47'10443 -- dc21

96-50110
CIP

MARLOR PRESS, INC.

4304 Brigadoon Drive   Saint Paul MN 55126

CONTENTS

47 Mariner's New York

Manhattan is an island, a historic seaport, and mariner's
territory. For people who like boats and the romance of the water,
here are six half-day tours you can do on your own,
ranging from a cruise around the island of Manhattan,
a dinner on a restaurant-yacht, and a visit to the
Intrepid Sea-Air-Space Museum and its famous ships.
Walk along the historic Battery,
take a ferry ride to the Statue of Liberty, and enjoy
an evening sail on a yacht. Visit the fabulous South Street Seaport
Museum and tread the decks of fabulous four-masted ships.
Eat at seaport restaurants. You don't have to be
a sailor to enjoy this custom tour.

67 Romantic New York

You think the Big Apple isn't romantic? Then join us for a
horse-drawn carriage ride, charming restaurants, romantic artists,
gorgeous views and superb music. Maybe even take a
gondola ride. Perhaps no other city has more for travelers with
romance in their souls — if they know where to look for it.

87 Shopper's New York

Manhattan is a shopper's paradise, whether you are in town
looking for something stylish from an elegant store, looking for a
bargain (and does New York have these!) or prepared to spend a
king or queen's ransom. Here's a wide-swinging, if somewhat
opinionated, look at the wide world of shopping in New York,
ranging from Bloomingdale's to Tiffany's. Bring money.

109 Art Lover's New York

The author apologizes a little for this set of three-day (or six half
day) tours, recognizing that in a city with more than 150 museums
and 400 art galleries, the tours are little more than an appetizer.
Yet here is, arguably, a discriminating way to see
in a short period of time the very best
of Manhattan museums and art collections.

133 Gardens of New York

New York is wall-to-wall skyscrapers, right? Take another look, for within Manhattan are many wonderful open spaces, atriums, and gardens, sometimes in surprising spots. Some of these are the best kept secrets in Manhattan. Here's your chance to take a break and discover on your own some of these jewels in Manhattan's crown.

159 Jewish New York

Some of the energy, beauty, bustle, and color of Manhattan comes from the New York that is Jewish. Visit old synagogues, wonderful restaurants, shops and historic landmarks in this colorful, not-to-be forgotten series of tours on your own. Quick tip: Bring an appetite. Try warm bialys.

177 Children's New York

Leave the children at home when you visit New York? Heavens, no! The author presents a special tour of New York that appeals especially to children. The author draws on her own experiences with a young grandson. New York, she says, can be even more extraordinary when you see it through the eyes of a child.

193 Mini-Walks through Manhattan

New York has a number of places which are fascinating to explore, but which did not fit into the larger chapters. Here are some of the author's favorite half day tours of Battery Park City, Union to Madison Squares, East Village and fascinating Chelsea. These mini-walks are easy to do, are complete with history and explanations, and, of course, provide step-by-step maps.

209 Index

MAP OF NEW YORK

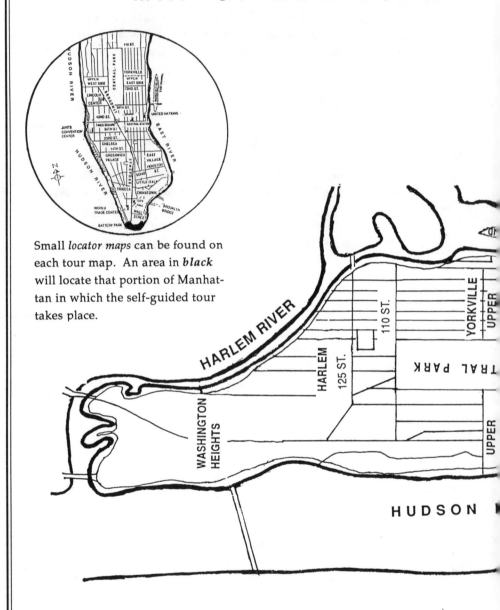

Small *locator maps* can be found on
each tour map. An area in **black**
will locate that portion of Manhattan in which the self-guided tour
takes place.

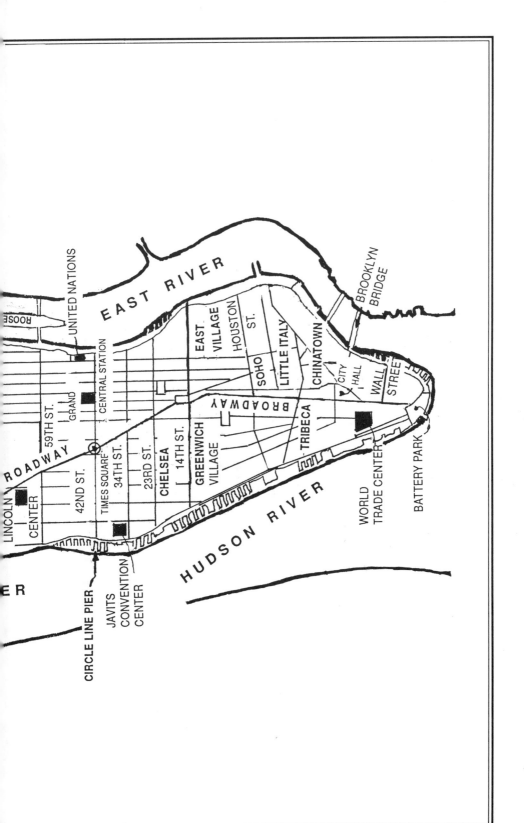

MAPS
& FLOOR PLANS

GUIDE
TO
ILLUSTRATIONS

Introduction

Manhattan, one of the five boroughs which make up New York City, is one of the most exciting, diverse, energizing, frustrating, difficult, noisy, dirty, and glorious places in the whole world.

You have heard of the glories of the city, from the Statue of Liberty's raised torch and Ellis Island to the Metropolitan Museum's medieval Cloisters at the north end of this twelve-mile-long island. You have also heard the horror stories of bankruptcy, muggings, drug dealings and filthy, dangerous subways. The truth is that all the stories are true.

It is important to plan your trip to maximize the positive and minimize the negative. Knowing your way around any city is useful; knowing your way around Manhattan is essential. With a minimum amount of effort, you can avoid most of the pitfalls inherent in a large city and enjoy its exhilarating treasures. This book will provide you with just that kind of knowledge about the layout of the city, how to get to places easily, and how to plan your visit to get the most out of your explorations.

I have tried to be as accurate as possible, but I know there will be changes by the time this revised book is published. Probably no place in the world changes more rapidly than Manhattan, so if the restaurant is closed or the telephone number has changed or the building has been torn down, just remember it is precisely this dynamism which attracted you in the first place.

Each chapter is aimed at people with a specific interest, but there is no reason why various day's interests cannot be mixed and matched. You can easily take a tour from one chapter and then do another half-day tour from another chapter. The day tours are planned for the energetic who are in the city to sightsee, not for leisurely vacationers. These walks can be managed by folks who start early, stick to the proposed schedules, and want to see a good bit of the city in a limited amount of time.

A word about restaurants in this book: I have tried to select restaurants which have been in Manhattan for a long time and are places which are unique to this city. Restaurants come and go in this town like lemmings to the sea, but there are some which manage to survive, year after year.

In some instances, I have suggested alternatives to expensive selections. Personally, my favorite spots to eat here are the delis, because no place has been able to duplicate either the food or the ambience of a New York deli.

No city in the world has so many fascinating places crammed into such a small place as you will find in Manhattan. You could live here a lifetime and never see it all. These walks will only whet your appetite for more visits and explorations of this urban wonderland.

One final note of thanks to my friends and family who helped make this book possible. My love and thanks to my late husband, Dick, who not only drew all the maps that illustrate the book, but encouraged and applauded all my efforts. Special thanks to Ellen and her cohorts, Andrea, Candace, Sharon, Debbie and Tom, who provided me office space, the use of a word processor and constant help; to my daughter, Ruth, my grandson, John, and my friends, Liz and Becky, who shared their homes and good cheer during my extended stays in New York when I began writing this book, and to all the rest of my family who provided steadfast support.

And finally, my deepest gratitude to my publisher, Marlin Bree, for his belief in my ability to write this book.

Ruth Humleker
New York City

Practical information

No major city in the world changes as rapidly as New York. Buildings are razed; new ones built; old ones renovated and whole sections of the city rearranged. Everywhere you look, major development is underway. Old **Times Square** is in the middle of major changes with the theatre renovation project; the **Jacob Javits Convention Center** now sits on 22 acres on the west side of town; and **Battery Park City** was built on 92 acres added to the island by landfill from the **World Trade Center** development.

The **South Street Seaport** historic district grows every year. New buildings for IBM, AT&T and almost every other alphabet corporation have mushroomed throughout town. And old buildings have undergone major restoration, such as the 20 million dollar renovation of the **Woolworth Building** which included the replacement of all 2,843 windows; and a face-lift for the **Chrysler Building** with new tower lighting designed by William Van Alen in 1930 but never previously installed. The tower, with its illuminated spire and arches, is now one of Manhattan's nighttime jewels.

Museums have undergone major changes. The **Museum of Modern Art** sold its air rights; the result is a 44-story building above the museum's six floors, which is now double its previous size. The **Metropolitan Museum of Art** opened the Henry R. Kravis wing and the Petrie European Sculpture Court in 1991. A renovated **Guggenheim Museum** opened in 1991 and the restored **Jewish Museum** opened in 1992.

Restaurants open and close almost overnight. I have tried to recommend places to eat which are not only unique to New York, but will still be in existence when you visit. The same theory applies to the shopping places, but don't be too surprised if some of them have closed or moved. Prices quoted for meals, tickets, boat rides and admissions are accurate at the time of publication, but increases are likely.

Look for changes everywhere. On the other hand, part of the excitement of the city is the vitality and energy which results in change.

Travel Safety

Don't do anything you wouldn't do at home. Yes, this is a big city with more than its share of crime, but with a little common sense you can reduce your chances of adding to the statistics.

Some friends recently spent a few days in New York and had room service in their hotel every night because they were afraid to venture out after dark. You might as well stay home. There are better ways to have a good and safe time in New York.

Leave your gold chains and fancy watches at home. Don't hold money or credit cards in your hand while waiting in line. Don't put your wallet in your back pocket. Carry your purse under your arm or wear the strap diagonally, over your head and under your arm.

Stick with the crowds; don't go wandering down dark, lonely streets. Stay out of the parks and subways at night. And don't play any of the three-card Monte (the old shell game with cards) or dice games on the streets; they are for suckers.

This is an exciting, boisterous city. Part of its fascination is a certain amount of danger, but you can enjoy its charm and stay safe by using your head.

When to Visit

Come to New York whenever you get the chance. If you have a choice, spring is beautiful; all the theatres, music, dance and art shows seem to open in the fall; and Christmas in New York is better than Disneyland.

The weather ranges from averages of 32 degrees in the winter to 95 degrees in the summer. My least favorite time is during the hot weeks in July and August. But since the whole city is air-conditioned in the summer and centrally heated in the winter, you can be reasonably comfortable almost any time.

What to take

Pack your good manners, enthusiasm and curiosity; then think about clothes. The walking tours in this book demand comfortable shoes. If your feet are in good condition, the rest of you will follow.

Lightweight running or walking shoes are the best invention since sliced bread. Because good walking shoes are usually not beautiful, I often wear slacks which cover them up a bit

I also tend to dress in layers: a cotton shirt, sweater, and rain-coat in spring and fall and a down-filled jacket and boots in the winter. I have to admit I usually also bring my fur coat to town since New York store clerks always treat me differently when I am in my mink. In the summer, a hat comes in handy to protect you from the sun. I always tuck a folding umbrella in my large tote bag, just in case.

Remember, in the winter the buildings are often over-heated and in the summer, often overcooled by air-conditioning. If you plan to go on some of the boat trips suggested in this book, take binoculars and a scarf for your head. It is always a bit cooler on the water, so dress accordingly.

A few restaurants require men to wear a jacket and tie. I have made note of those places in the book. Most women can get by for most occasions with a simple suit or dress, but if you want to dress up, this is the place to do it.

Take about half the clothes you think you will need, and bring extra money. Remember, this is the shopping capital of the world. Don't shop before you come; buy it here.

Airport Transportation

You will fly into **John F. Kennedy International Airport,** known as JFK, **La Guardia Airport** or **Newark International Airport.** Taxis serve all three airports. Fares will be about $30 from JFK to midtown Manhattan, around $30 from La Guardia, and $35 or more from Newark. You pay all bridge tolls, about $3.50, plus a surcharge of 50 cents per bag.

Look for the cab dispatcher at the airport and use only the yellow cabs, licensed by the city. Do not take any other kind of taxi. The so-called gypsy cabs, who may try to hustle you inside the terminal, often overcharge and sometimes take passengers on circuitous routes to their destination. A tip of 15 per cent is expected, a bit more if the driver is particularly helpful.

There are cheaper rides into town. All terminals are served by buses which operate between the airports and a number of midtown locations. From JFK or La Guardia airports, the **Carey Transportation** buses will take you to the **East Side Airlines Terminal**, from where you can get a cab to your hotel. The fare is about $7.50. Service runs from 5 a.m. until midnight, leaving every half hour. The La Guardia trip takes from 30-50 minutes; the JFK trip 45 minutes to an hour. For information call (718) 632-0500.

Newark airport is served by the **New Jersey Transit** between the airport and the **Port Authority Bus Terminal** at Eighth Ave. and 41st St. in Manhattan. Buses run every 15 minutes from

5:00 a.m. until about midnight, every 30 minutes from 1 a.m. to 5 a.m. The fare is about $7.50. Travel time is half an hour. Take a cab from the bus terminal to your hotel. For information call 762-5100. Incidentally the bus terminal has recently been rejuvenated and is considerably more pleasant than it used to be, but don't hang around. This is one of the more unpleasant parts of town, not untypical of bus station locations in many cities.

If you should come into town by bus, you will arrive at the same **Port Authority Bus Terminal** in Manhattan. Your point of entry by train will probably be either **Pennsylvania Station** between Seventh and Eighth Avs., 31st - 33rd Sts. or **Grand Central Terminal** at Park Ave. and 42nd St. Taxis are available outside the bus terminal and both train stations.

If you decide to come by car, your hotel doorman can direct you to either the hotel parking garage or nearby facilities. Take my advice and don't come by car. Parking is incredibly expensive, tow away zones are numerous and meter maids and tow trucks are just waiting for you. The traffic is horrendous and the streets even worse. Fly, bus or train, but don't drive. Your car will prove to be an albatross around your vacation.

Traveling in New York

The best way to get around any city is by foot and New York is no exception. This book contains walking tours, augmented by an occasional cab, bus or subway ride. Although there are thousands of places to see, this island is only twelve miles long and two and a half miles across. You can walk most of it. It is by far the finest way to see the city.

A few tips on how the city is arranged. North of 14th St., Manhattan is laid out in a grid system, except for Broadway which runs diagonally across the whole city. Fifth Ave. is the dividing line between east and west streets. Remember the Hudson River is on the west and the East River on the east. Easy?

The smallest building numbers are closest to Fifth Ave. One-way traffic usually goes east on even-numbered streets and west on odd-numbered streets, although there are some exceptions. Two-way traffic is on some crosstown streets, including 14th, 34th, 42nd, 57th and 72nd.

North and south streets are either numbered or bear names such as Madison, Park and Lexington. Sixth Ave. is officially known as Avenue of the Americas. A New Yorker calls it Sixth Avenue.

Traffic is one-way on most north and south streets; again there are exceptions such as Park Ave. with two-way traffic. Although north/south streets are parallel, the building numbers do not correspond from one block to another. For example a 200 number on Madison may be a 700 number a block over on Park.

When you are looking for an address, always ask for the nearest cross street. It will save you lots of time and shoe leather. There is a very complicated system for finding out the location of building numbers in New York. On a short visit, take my advice and ask for the cross street.

Incidentally, 20 north/south blocks are equal to a mile. It takes about one minute to walk a block, if you aren't stopping to window shop. The east/west blocks are twice as long as the north/south ones.

South of 14th St., it is every man for himself. The grid pattern disappears; bring out your maps. The streets follow the old Indian paths, trout streams, and cow trails in Greenwich Village and the Battery. I hope our maps will simplify the walks through lower Manhattan.

Incidentally, to New Yorkers, Uptown means north, Downtown is south, and Crosstown is east or west.

Taxis. With more than 11,000 licensed cabs in town, taxis are usually easily available, fast but expensive for the short-term visitor to the city. Most cabs cruise; the lighted sign on top indicates the cab is available. Avoid the gypsy cabs; just hail the yellow cabs. Stand on the curb, raise your arm or your umbrella and hope for the best. Do not stand on the curb and ask the driver if he will take you wherever you are going. Get in the cab and then tell the driver your destination. Cabs are plentiful except after the theater or when it rains. If you have a problem, walk to the nearest hotel and tip the doorman to get you a cab. Currently, cab rates are $2 per one-eighth mile, 50 cents for each one-fifth mile.

Pay your fare before you leave the cab, unless you have luggage in the trunk. Double check to make sure you have your purse, packages, coats and other belongings before you get out. One night in a rush to get to the theater, I left my purse in the cab and chased the cab down the street, yelling like a banshee. Fortunately, the driver heard me and stopped; I did not get run over in the process. It is not an occasion I would care to repeat.

Subways and buses. The best way to learn the subway and bus systems is to get maps in advance of your trip and spend some time studying them. Write the **New York Convention and Visitors Bureau**, 2 Columbus Circle at West 59th St., New York, N.Y., 10019 or send a self-addressed, stamped business size envelope to **New York City Transit Authority**, Customer Services Room 875, 370 Jay St., Brooklyn, N.Y., 11201. Maps are often out of print, but if they have them, they will send them to you. For additional subway and bus information call (718) 330-1234. Travel information specialists are on duty 24 hours a day.

You will be told that maps are available at subway stations. That is one of the many urban myths they tell in New York. If you do not get maps before your trip, pick them up at the Visitors Bureau at Columbus Circle or 42nd St.

If you still have problems, which you undoubtedly will, ask for help at the ticket booths or from other riders. You will probably get more information than you really want. New Yorkers, contrary to public opinion, love to give directions.

Buses. Cheap, slow and great for sightseeing, except during rush hours. You need exact change or a subway token, available at the toll booths in subway stations. Incidentally, token clerks do not accept bills larger than $20. Currently a ride costs $1.50. Your bus transfers are free; if you need one, ask when you get on the bus. Buses stop every two blocks going north and south and every block going crosstown; look for the bus signs. To get off, either press the tape on the bus wall or pull the bell cord.

Subways. Fast, cheap, dirty and complicated. Study the subway map, ask questions or call the Visitors Bureau, 397-8200. Tokens cost $1.50. A fare increase for subways is under consideration at this writing. Tickets can be bought singly or in packets of 10 (Ten-Paks), no discount. One of the trickiest things about riding the subway is to find the entrances. On a good day, the stairways are marked by lighted globes; unfortunately, these often are not working.

Notice that express and local trains run on the same lines. If you are not sure where the express stops, just take the local train. It won't take much longer and it beats having to take a long ride back into the city.

If you choose not to use the subways, you are missing a unique New York experience. The old trains are gradually being replaced by new, air-conditioned ones on most of the lines. In the summer always look for the cars with closed windows; those are the air-conditioned ones.

And yes, it is sometimes dangerous to ride the subways. I advise a visitor to stay out of the subways at rush hours because they are so crowded, and after dark when the muggers and pickpockets get busy.

Visitor Centers

The New York Convention and Visitors Bureaus are located at 2 Columbus Circle and 229 W. 42nd St., between 7th and 8th Sts. For telephone information, call 397-8200. They are open Monday to Friday, 9 a.m. to 6 p.m.

You can get a city guide and map, guides for restaurants, hotels and shopping, bus and subway maps, tickets to television shows and theater tickets called "two-fers", short for "two for the price of one." These can be exchanged at theatre box offices for half-price tickets. The theatre tickets are available on a day-to-day, first-come, first-served basis. Pick up folders listing guided tours, boat trips and special services such as baby-sitting. The multi-lingual staff will answer questions, give advice and generally try to make your visit as pleasant as possible.

Theater Information

Theater in New York falls into three categories: Broadway, Off-Broadway and Off-Off Broadway. Broadway theater is the commercial, establishment theater located near and around Times Square. Here you will find the big hits, the big stars, the high-priced and often hard-to-get tickets.

Off-Broadway theater began with groups such as the **Provincetown Players** in Greenwich Village. These theaters present new, often experimental productions. The theaters are small, usually seating under 300 people and located in out-of-the-way spots in the city.

Off-Off-Broadway theater is even more avant garde than the Off-Broadway productions. Many of these groups are located in cafes, warehouses, churches and lofts. When my actor-son appeared in his first Off-Off-Broadway show, *A Comedy of Errors,* I remember hoping the title of the play was not an editorial comment on his career. Actually this theater was located Off-Off-The-Bowery. I remember standing outside the theater-warehouse after the show, watching people throw bottles out of the second floor windows of the surrounding buildings. A few minutes later, the theater manager came outside with a straight-backed chair, set it down, climbed up on it and removed the one unshaded electric light bulb which advertised the show and took it inside. For the first time, I think I understood something about Off-Off. You will have some extraordinarily wonderful and also some awful experiences in these theaters.

Tickets. You can order through ticket brokers at home or in New York; you can buy at the theater box-offices; and you can purchase by phone from **Telecharge** 239-6200, or **Ticketron,** 246-0102 24-hours a day, 7 days a week, if you have a major credit card. Both charge extra fees.

If you want to save money, try **TKTS,** the Times Square Ticket Center at W. 47th St. Each day half-price tickets are made available for some plays for that day's performances. Near the ticket booths are posted a list of the plays for which tickets are available. The lines may look long, but there are six windows in operation and they move right along. The last time I stood in line, it took exactly fifteen minutes to reach the ticket seller, and that was on a weekend. The booths are open Monday through Saturday, from 11 a.m. to 5:30 p.m., for tickets to same-day evening performances. For matinee performances, tickets are available on Wednesday and Saturday from noon to 2 p.m., and for Sunday matinee and evening performances, from noon to 8 p.m. Another TKTS booth at the **World Trade Center** in Lower Manhattan sells half-price tickets for evening performances only. The lines are usually shorter here.

The Public Theater, 425 Layfayette, sells "Rush " tickets for $15 to $20 thirty minutes before performances.

Many other theaters do not have a formal policy, but often release house seats shortly before curtain time.

However you get your tickets, do plan to go to the theater during your visit. Broadway, The Great White Way, can be wonderful, but also try one of the more unconventional performances for a very special New York experience.

Music and dance performances are abundant, ranging from classical to rock; from jazz to punk; from the waltz to ballet to disco or whatever the latest fad is. Consider a performance at the **Metropolitan Opera, Carnegie Hall, City Ballet** or any of the hundreds of small clubs, churches or Y's in town.

The music and dance ticket booth is located in Bryant Park,

West 42nd St. between Fifth and Sixth Avs. for same day evening performances. It is open Tuesday, Thursday and Friday from noon to 2 p.m., and 3 to 7 p.m.; Wednesday and Saturday from 11 a.m. to 2 p.m., and 3 to 7 p.m.; Sunday from noon to 6 p.m. Monday tickets are sold on Sunday.

Concert and dance tickets are also available from brokers, telephone credit exchanges or at the box office. Check the daily newspapers or weekly New York or New Yorker magazines for current listings.

Tipping

Porters expect $1 per bag; coat checkers, 50 cents; and taxi drivers about 15 percent of the fare. The easiest way to figure the tip in a restaurant is to double the 8 1/4 percent tax on your bill. I suspect that is how the city figured out how much sales tax to levy. Of course, tipping is for acceptable service: remember TIPS is an acronym for "To insure Prompt Service."

Bed & Breakfasts

I have not attempted to provide information about hotels in this book, but I recently came across an unusual affordable and very nice bed and breakfast operation in New York City: Off Park Bed and Breakfast. All the apartments are located in the heart of Manhattan. They are fully furnished, including cable television and answering machines, as well as full kitchen facilities, complete with breakfast provisions and many other personal touches.

There is a three-night minimum stay and a 25 percent deposit required to reserve a booking. Deposits can be refunded up to 10 days prior to arrival. The balance in either cash or traveler checks is made on arrival. To reserve, call the host at (212) 228-4645.

Booking rates range from $15 to $115 for 1 or 2 persons, plus $15 per additional guest. This can be a very nice way for couples or families to "live" in New York.

Helpful Telephone Numbers

Emergency: Dial 911

Alcoholics Anonymous: For advice and help in locating a meeting 647-1680

Dental Emergency Service: 679-3966 24 hours, 679-4172 after 8 p.m.

Doctors on Call: 718-238-2100

24 hour Drugstore: 755-2266 Kaufman's/50th and Lexington

Gay/Lesbian Switchboard: 777-1800 6 a.m. to midnight

New York Convention & Visitors Bureau: 397-8200

Time: 976-1616

Weather: 976-1212

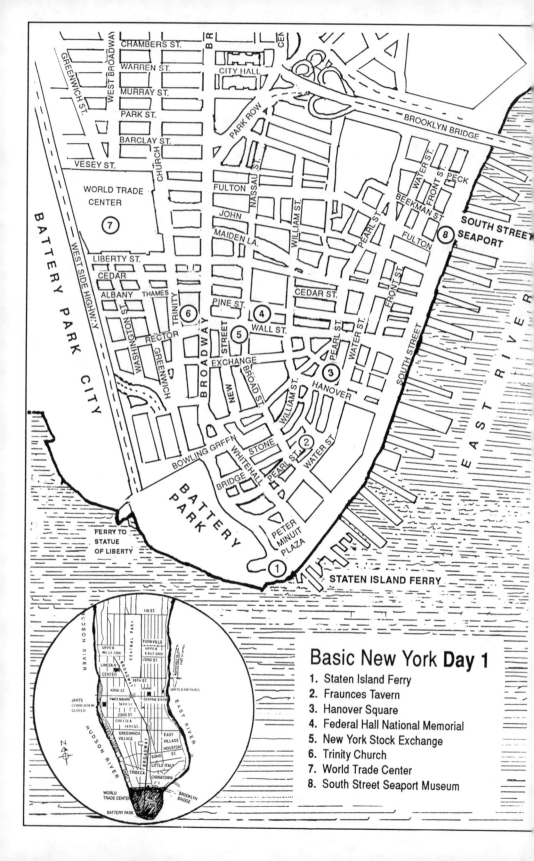

Basic New York Day 1

1. Staten Island Ferry
2. Fraunces Tavern
3. Hanover Square
4. Federal Hall National Memorial
5. New York Stock Exchange
6. Trinity Church
7. World Trade Center
8. South Street Seaport Museum

Basic Three Days
in New York

A three-day tour of New York will give you a quick look at the diversity, size and excitement of the city. You will move from south to north, just as the city grew. Beginning at the foot of the island, you will see the **Statue of Liberty,** just as every new arrival saw her as their boats entered the harbor. You will walk through the financial district, get a view of the city from the tallest building in town and tour the renovated site of the old ports of New York.

The second day you will make your way through the ethnic enclaves of **Chinatown** and **Little Italy,** visit the galleries and shops in Soho and wander through **Greenwich Village** before seeing an **Off-Broadway play.** The third day you will move up-town to **Rockefeller Center** and **St. Patrick's Cathedral,** stop at the **Museum of Modern Art,** visit some of New York's grand stores and end the afternoon with the quickest tour of the enormous **Metropolitan Museum of Art** which I could devise, consistent with the time constraints.

And after all that, you will have barely touched the treasures of this incredible city. My hope is that it will give you a taste for more.

Day 1

Highlights: Staten Island Ferry, Wall Street, Trinity Church, World Trade Center and the **South Street Seaport**.

Reservations: Reserve theater tickets for a **Broadway play**. Either order tickets in advance and pay full price, or take a chance at the **half-price booth** you will visit today at the World Trade Center.

Lunch: Greenhouse Cafe, World Trade Center. *Telephone 444-4010,* or **Windows on the World Restaurants.** *phone 524-7000.*

For supper after the theater: Joe Allen, 326 W. 46th St., *Telephone 581-6464.*

Morning

Start your day's tour where New York originated: at the foot of the island. Take a cab, a bus or a subway to **Battery Park** and the **Staten Island Ferry** pier.

Plan to take the **9 a.m. ferry** in order to be back about 10 a.m. for your walk toward **Wall Street** and the **World Trade Center**. The **Staten Island Ferry** runs 24 hours a day, 7 days a week. Time tables change, but usually the ferry runs every 20 minutes from 7:30 a.m. and on weekends every 1/2 hour from 9:30 a.m. to 9:30 p.m.; then every hour. If you want to be absolutely certain about times, call 806-6940, but it is not necessary. The round trip takes about one hour for the 5-mile trip.

Colonel Cornelius Vanderbilt's fortune began with his ownership of the Staten Island Ferry. Since the price is still only 50 cents each way at this writing, it is hard to figure out how he got so rich. This may be the cheapest hour you spend in Manhattan. The ferry looks big and awkward, but she is sturdy and effective.

I think this is the fastest, least expensive and best way to see the skyline of the city, the ports and islands, bridges and hills of

Staten Island and the lady herself, Liberty.

It is one of the great boat rides in the world and will give you a real sense of why the first immigrants settled here. The magnificent harbor, ports, and access to the sea are dramatic. To your right, as you move out toward Staten Island, is the renovated **Statue of Liberty.** The lady still lights the way to freedom as she did when Bartholdi, the Alsatian sculptor, designed her. France gave us the 151-foot sculpture; with a considerable amount of prodding from Joseph Pulitzer and his New York World newspaper; Americans came up with the money for the 89-foot pedestal. President Grover Cleveland dedicated her on October 28, 1886. The more recent $200 million renovation should keep her shining for another 100 years.

Near the statue is **Ellis Island,** the processing center for more than 17 million immigrants, many as recently as 1950. The newly restored Ellis Island opened to the public again in the fall of 1990. After eight years and $156 million, the gleaming building and well-kept grounds are worth visiting on a longer trip.

On your left is **Governor's Island,** where the U.S. Coast Guard is located.It is only open twice a year, on Open House days. When the ferry turns around, you are facing the extraordinary panorama of the city's skyline. It doesn't seem to make any difference what the weather; the view is always dramatic. As you pass the ocean-going ships waiting for berths or anchored tankers, the city beckons you back. Many people love the overcast days when the foghorns are braying and buildings move out of the mist like great ships. In the morning, you may have sunshine gilding the massive buildings or rain falling in drops on the downtown skyscrapers, but whatever the weather, you will be drawn back to the city as though you already knew and loved her.

The **Staten Island** ferry slip is just to the east of **Battery Park.** As you disembark and start to walk up Whitehall St., which is just a short few steps to the right of the landing, look to your left toward **Battery Park.** There you will see **Castle Clinton,** built in 1811 as a fortress, now housing a museum, information center, and ticket booths for boat trips to the Statue of Liberty. This fortification helped defend the harbor during the War of 1812, and later served as an entertainment center where Jenny Lind sang and General Lafayette was feted. From 1855 to 1890, it served as an immigrant depot for more than seven million people.

Walk up **Whitehall St.** On your left you will pass a flagpole which is a monument to New York's first Jewish immigrants, 23 men, women and children, who landed here in 1654. Just beyond, on the left, is **Peter Minuit Plaza**, named for the Dutch governor who, in 1626, purchased the island of Manhattan from the Indians for $24 worth of trinkets. The Indians called this land Man-a-hat-ta, meaning Heavenly Land.

Turn right on **Pearl St.**, which will take you to the Fraunces Tavern block of 18th and 19th-century buildings, located at the corner of Broad and Pearl Sts. **Fraunces Tavern**, at 54 Pearl St., is a reconstruction of a mansion built in 1719 for Stephen De Lancey, later purchased by Samuel Fraunces in 1763. It was here Fraunces opened the Queen's Head Tavern. He was Chief Steward to George Washington. It was in the tavern's Long Room that General Washington bid farewell to his officers in 1783. A restaurant and small museum are now located here. Take a few minutes to climb the stairs to the second floor museum and shop. The shop is filled with charming merchandise, wonderful books and at last visit, a delightful young manager.

Continue up Pearl St., once paved with oyster shells, another reminder of how close this area was to the water. Pass India House and **Hanover Square** on your left. Here you will find **William Bradford's Printing House**, with the first printing press in the colony, and at 199 Pearl St., the house in which Captain Kidd lived. He was later hanged as a pirate, though that may not have been the case.

Continue up Pearl St. to **Wall Street**: The Street. You are now at the site of the old Dutch city gate and the foot of Wall St. In

1653, a wall of wooden planks was built across the island on this stretch of road to protect the settlers from Indians, the British and whoever else might attack. It didn't do much good, since the inhabitants kept stealing the planks for firewood. In 1655, 500 Indians invaded, rioted, looted the village and then attacked the surrounding farms. In 1699, the wall was finally torn down.

From this corner you see the famous view of this fabled street. The old wooden planks have been replaced by a wall of banks and office buildings. This is indeed the canyon of New York.

Look to its far end; the newly cleaned spire and gold numbers on the clock dial of **Trinity Church** will draw you down this street of power and money.

Walk on to the **Federal Hall National Memorial** with the enormous statue of George Washington standing in front. Washington was inaugurated here in 1789 and John Quincy Adams Ward's sculpture commemorates that event. The steps are usually filled with young people taking the sun, eating and talking. Climb the steep steps to explore this historic building. Free 20-minute guided tours are offered at half hour intervals. The building is open from 9 a.m. to 5 p.m., Monday through Friday, year-round and on weekends during the summer months. For additional information, call 825-6888.

Number 8 Broad St., just around the corner from Wall Street, is home to the famous, sometimes infamous, **New York Stock Exchange.** The visitor's entrance is actually at 20 Broad St. Free tickets for self-guided tours are distributed daily outside 20 Broad St. for same-day 45-minute periods. Tickets are available at 9 a.m. The Visitor's gallery is open from 9:15 a.m. to 4 p.m., weekdays. Security is tight here; they searched my handbag, x-rayed my camera and walked me through a security gate.

The Stock Exchange floor can be quiet or mad, depending on the amount of trading. Earphones are available for translation of information about the Exchange in French, Spanish, German and Japanese.

Note the buttonwood tree in front of the building. The new tree was planted in 1992, the 200-year anniversary of The Stock Exchange. It is a reminder of the 1790s when 24 brokers transacted business outdoors in good weather, under the tree. A handshake was their contract.

(6) You have reached the west end of Wall St. and **Trinity Church**, the third church to stand on this site. The first one burned to the ground in 1776; the second was torn down because of structural weaknesses. The present Gothic revival building with its brownstone exterior was completed in 1846. Trinity Church and the adjoining cemetery are open daily. Note the bell tower with its 280-foot spire and the bronze doors modeled after the Ghiberti doors of the Baptistry in Florence, Italy. Inside be sure to notice the gorgeous stained glass behind the carved altar wall. A small museum is located to the left of the altar.

The **church cemetery** contains the remains of 1,186 people, including many of the early Dutch settlers. The oldest grave is that of Richard Churcher, age 5, who died in 1681. It is located to the right of the church. Many of the stones indicate the horrors of that time with mentions of plagues, smallpox, cholera and other diseases.

Among the famous folk buried here are William Bradford, age 92 (1752), who began New York's first newspaper and was the father of the free press in the United States; Captain James Lawrence, Commander of the Chesapeake during the War of 1812 and remembered for his cry, "Don't give up the ship;" and Alexander Hamilton, U.S. Secretary of the Treasury and loser in the duel with Aaron Burr. Look for Robert Fulton's monument by the Rector St. fence. You will remember him as the inventor of the steamboat, but his tombstone contains a self-portrait, a memory of his earlier years as a painter.

Return to **Broadway** and walk north past the **Equitable** and the **Marine Midland Bank** buildings on your right. You cannot fail to notice the gigantic red **Cube** by Noguchi, balanced on one corner. The 28-foot structure required a building permit because it was considered an "enclosed mass," whatever that is.

Turn left at The Cube to **Liberty St.** and you will be facing the base of Manhattan's **World Trade Center** with its huge twin ⑦ towers, a five-acre plaza and 50,000 people at work. An additional 80,000 visitors and business people come to the center each day. In 1993, a bomb exploded at the World Trade Center, causing enormous damage. Although the devastation has mostly been repaired, there have been many changes, including the ownership of the hotel and other entities, a multi-million dollar renovation of the restaurants and bars on the top floors, and, of course increased security.

The complex includes two 110-story high buildings, commonly referred to as the **Twin Towers**, three low buildings and the 22-story Marriott World Trade Center Hotel, all of which circle the five-acre plaza. The buildings are connected at ground level by a walking concourse and shopping hall. The 2,000-car parking garage, a city subway and PATH railway lines are underground. Shops and restaurants are located throughout the concourse and upper floors. Restaurants range from fast food bars to one of the most elegant and expensive restaurants in New York, Windows on the World, Cellars in the Sky, and a bar on the 106th and 107th floors.

Just west of the World Trade Center is the largest planned urban development project in the country, **Battery Park City.** The 100-acre site was created by removing unused piers and filling the space with material from the World Trade Center excavation. It is a town with a working population of 31,000 and a residential population of 30,000. Architect Cesar Pelli designed this newest miracle in a city of miracles, and in the process, provided people access to a new section of the Hudson River, long denied.

Lunch

Enter **Two World Trade Center** from Liberty St. and walk through the building to One World Trade Center and the Marriott Hotel, where you can have lunch in the **Greenhouse Cafe.** This is one of the prettiest restaurants in this part of town, with breakfasts and lunch buffets. A bit pricey.

Afternoon

After lunch, return to **Two World Trade Center**. Take the escalator to the mezzanine level. Check for **TKTS**, the booth selling half-price tickets for Broadway and Off Broadway shows for same-day evening performances. It is open Monday through Friday, from 11:30 a.m. to 5:30 p.m.; on Saturday, from 11 a.m. to 3 p.m. Check the length of the line to determine whether you want to spend time here to buy discounted tickets. This ticket booth is rarely as crowded as the one just off 42nd St. No credit cards, only cash or traveler's checks.

Walk out onto the plaza just off the mezzanine level. Note the sculpture strategically located, including Fritz Koenig's bronze **Globe**, James Rosati's **Ideogram** and Nagare's black granite pyramid at the main entrance. A Calder stabile is on the west side of the North Tower. For a slightly disorienting but exciting view, let your eyes follow the silver columns on the exterior of the building upward to the sky. The building seems to move.

Tickets for the **observation roof** are available on the mezzanine. Elevators will whisk you to the glass enclosed observation deck on the 107th floor. Don't do this on a foggy, rainy or windy day. The fog and rain will inhibit your view. On windy days the building sways alarmingly. If weather permits, you can take an escalator from the 107th floor to the 110th floor for the rooftop promenade. The observation decks are open 9:30 a.m. to 9:30 p.m. daily.

This is one of the most extraordinary views you will ever see. According to one advertisement you can see "7 bridges, 6 rivers, 5 boroughs, 4 stadiums, 3 airports, 2 states and 1 very beautiful city." The lightning-fast elevators make the trip in 58 seconds flat.

One suggestion: Some evening you may want to come back here as it begins to get dark and the city turns on its lights. For a reasonable amount of money you can have a drink and appetizers at what they call "The Greatest Bar On Earth." The view of the lights in the harbor, in the city and on the Statue of

Liberty is an experience I can assure you will be indelible.

Hail a cab in front of the Trade Center and ask to be taken to the
South Street Seaport. It is on the East River at the foot of Ful- ⑧
ton St. You could walk, but after your busy morning, relax and
take a short cab ride. It should cost about $5.

New York's ports, trade and commerce were centered on the
East River, an arm of the sea on the lee side of the island. It is
less affected than the Hudson River by ice, flooding and the
prevailing westerlies. The port of New York grew in impor-
tance during the 18th-century. Peter Schermerhorn built housing here for seamen and merchants, made goods for sea and
domestic trade, and provided office space for counting houses.
The Schermerhorn family also set up regular service to and
from Charleston. In 1814, a ferry service to Brooklyn from
Beekman's Slip began, and in 1822, the first Fulton Market
opened.

The Erie Canal, built in 1824, brought more than 500 new businesses here to handle all the new activity. By the 1850s, the
seaport was overwhelmed with the China trade and regular
packet service to Europe. It was the busiest port in America and
one of the richest.

As the 19th-century came to a close, things changed. Steam
replaced sail and the big new steamships found deepwater
berths on the Hudson River. The seaport diminished in impor-
tance, and by the 1950s, had fallen into disrepair. The Friends of
South Street Seaport began their rescue efforts in the 1960s. You
can now see the results. This is now one of the highlights of a
trip to New York. The 11-block district, which stretches from
Fulton St. to the Brooklyn Bridge, includes a museum, a collection of historic ships, galleries, a children's center, the restored
Schermerhorn row of shops and restaurants, and the Fulton
Market, which is located on what was once called Beekman
Slip. The seaport is open seven days a week. The museum is
open 10 a.m. to 5 p.m.; the ships close at 5 p.m.; shops at 9 p.m.,
and the restaurants are open until midnight.

Wander around and look at this remarkable place and recall **Walt Whitman's** words about it: "The countless masts, the white shore-steamers, the lighters, the ferry boats, the black steamers well-model'd." After your long walk this morning, you will be spending a leisurely afternoon exploring the seaport.

Ask your cab driver to deposit you at the corner of **Fulton and Front** Sts, near the lighthouse, built in memory of the victims of the 1912 **Titanic** disaster.

Walk down **Fulton St.** toward the river. You will pass **Schermerhorn Row** on your right, probably the most interesting buildings in the seaport area. They sit on the water lots purchased in 1793 by Peter Schermerhorn on the condition that they be filled in. This is the way much of this part of New York was created, by landfill of trash, bottles and debris from excavations.

Walk to the docks, purchase an admission ticket at the dockside booth, and visit one or more of the great sailing ships. The 321-foot **Peking** is one of the largest sailing ships ever built and one of the few square-riggers left in the world. The **Lettie G. Howard** is a wooden fishing schooner built in 1893; the English-built Wavertree is a square-rigged, iron-hulled ship.

The same company that runs the Circle Line cruises around Manhattan now runs the Seaport Liberty Cruises here. They offer a one-hour trip to the harbor south of Battery Park, passing the Statue of Liberty and Ellis Island. The cruises are offered from the middle of March through December. Schedules and ticket prices are subject to change, but currently in 1996 the tickets are $12 for adults, $10 for seniors and $6 for children 12 and under.

One of the most remarkable sights from the seaport is the view of one of New York's greatest engineering triumphs, the **Brooklyn Bridge,** the first bridge over the East River.

The great new three-story glass and steel **Pier 17 Pavilion** extends out toward the river. There are outdoor promenades on each floor and a magnificent top floor view of the bridges and the East River. The pavilion is a treasure house of shopping and eating.

Along the river, you will see the old **Fulton Fish Market** under and beyond the F.D.R. Drive. Built in 1907, it is still operating early in the morning, albeit on a much smaller scale than in its glory days.

Walk down South St. to Peck Slip to **Con Edison's Seaport Substation,** with what seems to be a view of a Federal Building and a glimpse of the **Brooklyn Bridge.** Actually this is one of the many three-dimensional murals by Richard Haas which you will find around the city. I happen to love these murals and I think you will, too. Back off a bit to really see the illusion and then look up to see the real bridge. Walk a block to **Water St.,** turn left and stop in the book and chart store and the printing shop.

By now, it is probably 5 or 5:30 p.m. Tonight I have suggested going to a play on Broadway. Instead of dinner before the theater, I recommend a snack here at the seaport, a cab ride to the theater district, a drink before the play and then a late supper at one of Broadway's famous hangouts for theatrical personages.

Evening

Walk back to **Pier 17,** escalate to the third floor and select your late afternoon snack or drink from the many places located there. If the weather is pleasant, take your refreshments out on the promenade, settle in one of the deck chairs and enjoy the late afternoon river sights.

After your rest, grab a cab and ask him (they are usually hims) to take you to **Times Square.** It should be about 6 or 6:30 p.m. Your Broadway theater, whichever one it is, will be within easy walking distance.

You will have time to explore the Times Square area a bit, have a drink, and still easily make your 8 p.m. curtain.

Times Square is where Broadway and Seventh Ave. intersect and is roughly bounded by 42nd and 48th Sts. It is crowded, neoned, tacky and exciting — and changing rapidly. As you stand in the triangle created by the intersection of Seventh Ave. and Broadway at 42nd St., just act like the tourist you are and gawk at all the neon, shops and Broadway characters.

Cross over to the other half of the Times Square oasis, in the middle of all the traffic, to **Father Duffy Square** to see the statue of the World War I hero. In front of him stands a statue of the entertainer, George M. Cohan, Broadway's Yankee Doodle Dandy.

At the corner of Times Square and 46th are two of the newest and biggest attractions in the area: the Virgin Megastore and the All Star Cafe. The Virgin Megastore has three floors filled with CDs, tapes, films, books, video screens and even a travel agency, Virgin Air, surprise, surprise. Next door is the enormous All Star Cafe where you can eat surrounded by 60 gigantic video screens showing a variety of sporting events. It is loud, glitzy and fun.

A few steps off the square is Virgil's barbecue restaurant. It is at 152 W. 44th St., between Broadway and 6th Av. It is also big and noisy and I like it. Its "pulled" pork sandwich with sides of slaw and potato salad for about $9 is fantastic. Do order at least one "southern" biscuit with maple sugar butter. It makes a great dessert.

Depending on your time, you might want to sit down and have a drink, coffee or a cola. On the east side of Times Square is an enormous McDonald's. It is filled with trees and glitz and Big Macs, but best of all it has a second floor with tables and chairs along a huge window overlooking Times Square. It is also filled with an extraordinary mix of New Yorkers. I happen to love sitting here, munching a cheeseburger, watching the sights and knowing I am in The City.

Or, you can walk down to 234 W. 44th St. to what many consider a tourist trap, **Sardi's** restaurant, filled with memories of star-studded nights and cartoons of all the greats who filled the tables.Just inside the door and to your left is a very nice, small bar with the most obliging bartenders I know in town.

Late night

After the theater, plan to have supper at one of the wonderful little places folks in the theater go for hamburgers or pasta.

My favorite is **Joe Allen's** at 326 W. 46th St. with its red and white checkered tablecloths. Reservations required, as I said earlier. Check the day's specials or just order your hamburger (with onions), and sit back and enjoy the show. Your waiter will be a starving actor working for the rent and anxious to rehearse a variety of roles with you; if you are patient, he or she will point out Liza Minnelli or whoever important comes in. These are the real gypsies of the theater world. I loved Joe Allen's in London and I love it in New York.

By this time of night you should have no difficulty getting a cab; they are all over the city. Back to your hotel to rest up for tomorrow.

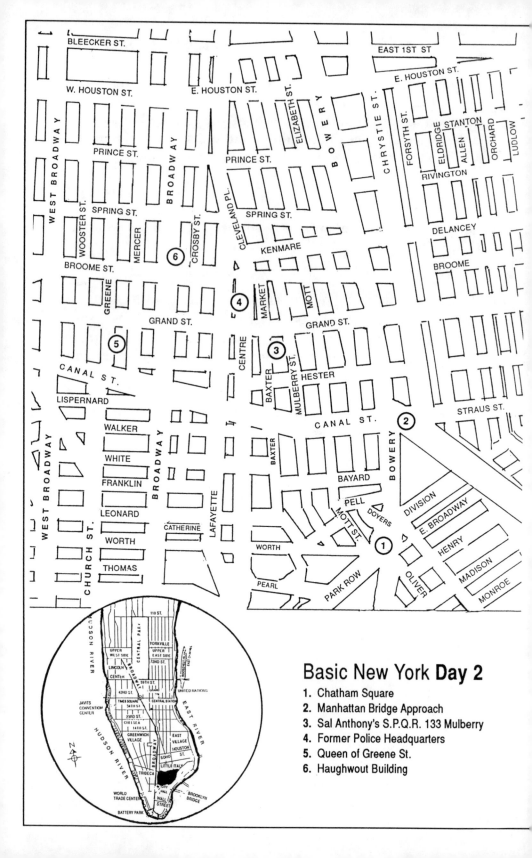

Basic New York **Day 2**

1. Chatham Square
2. Manhattan Bridge Approach
3. Sal Anthony's S.P.Q.R. 133 Mulberry
4. Former Police Headquarters
5. Queen of Greene St.
6. Haughwout Building

Day 2

Highlights: Chinatown, Little Italy, Soho, Greenwich Village, an **Off Broadway** play and a **jazz club**.

Reservations: Reserve tickets for an Off Broadway play, preferably in the Greenwich Village area.

Dinner reservations: Waverly Inn, 16 Bank St. at Greenwich Ave. Telephone 929-4377. Jazz Clubs **Village Vanguard,** 7th Ave. between 11th and Perry Sts. Telephone 255-4037 or **Blue Note,** 131 W. 3rd St. Telephone 475-8592.

Morning

Today's tour will start at **Chatham Square** about 10 a.m. The ①
square is just south of New York's **Chinatown,** which is one
of the largest Oriental communities in North America.
Chinatown "officially" is bounded by Canal, Worth and Baxter
Sts. and the Bowery, although it is nowspilling far beyond these
early limits.

Sunday is its busiest day, when former residents return to visit,
and people from all over the city come to shop. The relatively
tiny area is jammed with tenements, people, smells, noises and
great energy. But it is a far cry from the opium dens, gambling
houses, brothels and tong wars that characterised it at the turn
of the century.

Chinatown overflows with bustling shops and all kinds of
small businesses and suppliers. At any given moment there are
about 130 restaurants. Purveying food was one of the few businesses open to the Chinese at the turn of the century, since state
laws prohibited the Chinese from enterprises which competed
with Europeans.

Just a word about the wide variety of Oriental restaurants:
many of them will be just like the ones you eat in at home.
There are many Cantonese restaurants, but you will also find
the cooking of Shantung, Szechuan and Hunan, as well as spe-

cialized eating establishments. **Dim sum** parlors feature Chinese dumplings with various fillings. These are served on trays or rolling carts by the waiters. Just point to the ones you want and you will be billed according to the number of little dishes at your place. Noodle shops feature dishes with noodles in soup with meat or vegetables or fish. Rice houses are usually small and inexpensive, often just lunch counters, which serve a variety of toppings on rice. And finally there are the coffee shops which serve tea with rolls, cookies and conversation.

Now you are ready to start your stroll through Chinatown. **Chatham Square** is noisy, dirty and confusing. No wonder: Ten streets actually empty into the square. On the traffic island in the middle of all this mayhem, you will see the pagoda-style arch, the **Kim Lau Memorial**, dedicated in 1962 to the Chinese-Americans who died in the armed forces of the United States.

Just south of the Kim Lau Memorial is the **Shearith Israel Cemetery**. This is the earliest surviving burial ground of New York's first Jewish congregation. The oldest marker here is dated 1683.

Walk across the square, carefully, for the traffic is horrendous. Walk north on **Mott St.**, Chinatown's Main Street. Note the low tenements and the bright restaurant signs. Steps lead down into basement businesses, which were once gambling and opium dens. Tiny stores are crammed cheek by jowl: groceries, fish stands, tea stores, candy, ice cream and cookies. Look for all the Asian staples which are almost impossible to get anywhere else.

Turn right on Pell St. Number 16 is the **Buddhist Temple**, a joss house or prayer rooms. You are welcome to enter to see the altars replete with fruit, flowers, statues and burning incense. The low red lights cast a rosy glow.

Turn right onto **Doyers St.** which curves to the **Bowery**. The sharpest turn on Doyers is called *Dead Man's Curve* or *Bloody Angle*. At the turn of the century, this crook in the street was an ideal ambush spot. More murders occured here at that time than anywhere else in the United States. At the corner of the Bowery and Pell St. (Number 18 Bowery) notice the Edward Mooney House (1789), probably the oldest row house in Manhattan, now the Metro Communications Centre.

Walk north on the **Bowery**. Turn left to visit busy Bayard St., with its wonderful Chinatown Ice-cream Factory and its green tea, lichee, red bean, mango and other exotic flavors. Back to the Bowery and north to Canal St.

When you arrive at the corner of the **Bowery** and **Canal St.**, turn to your right to see the magnificent approach to the **Manhattan Bridge**. The Triumphal Arch was modeled after the 17th-century Porte St. Denis in Paris and the Colonnade after Bernini's at St. Peter's Square in Rome. Notice the granite sculpture flanking either side of the bridge and the frieze over the arch with Indians on horseback hunting buffalo. It was from here that Washington began his victory march into New York as the British fled.

Turn left and walk west on Canal St. about three blocks to **Mulberry St. Little Italy** is on the north side of Canal and Mulberry is its main street.

Turn right on **Mulberry St.**, with its Italian flags and little twinkling lights strung from the buildings, along with lines of washing and tinsel-draped restaurants.
At the corner of Mulberry and Hester is **Umberto's Clam Bar,** where the underworld figure Joey Gallo "got his."

Noon

Time for lunch and what better place to eat than in **Little Italy**. Continue walking north on Mulberry to *Sal Anthony's S.P.Q.R.*, with its Prix Fixe Lunch. Try the Arugala salad and the veal.

Save room for dessert at **Ferrara's**, a bakery and espresso bar at 195 Grand St., between Mulberry & Mott Sts. Have a cappucino with one of their good pastries. They have delicious ice cream creations including a wonderful tartufo: ice cream covered with a hard chocolate and a center of cherries.

Afternoon

(4) **W**alk west on Grand St. two blocks to **Center St.** A few steps to your right is the baroque former **Police Headquarters,** with its main entrance decorated with a New York coat of arms and five statues representing the five boroughs. It is very strange to see this elegant building sitting in the middle of all these tenements.

Continue west on Grand St. to **Greene St.** (about 6 or 7 blocks) with its 19th century block pavements. You are now in **SoHo,** the acronym for SOuth of HOuston (pronounced Howston by New Yorkers). In London, the area called SoHo derived its name from an old hunting call, but both SoHo's are home to artists, writers, filmmakers, musicians, and other free spirits.

In 1962, the City Club of New York published a study of this 26-block section and called it "the wastelands of New York City" with "no buildings worth saving." For the traffic engineers who were planning an expressway through the neighborhood, this was a bonanza. But the study brought instant reaction from architects, artists, university professors and newspapers. In 1973, SoHo was designated a historic district and the handsome cast iron buildings were saved.

It was these extraordinary buildings which saved the area from demolition. Built between 1860 and 1890, these early cast iron buildings were designed to imitate stone; some were painted to resemble marble or limestone. As you walk around SoHo, you will notice the remarkable columns, cornices, arches, bays, pediments and scrollwork. If you want to be sure the building is cast-iron, carry a little magnet with you and toss it up against the building. If it sticks, you will know.

Artists had been creeping into the area for years, usually somewhat surreptitiously, after discovering the great open spaces with huge windows, just right for the monumental paintings and sculpture that were then underway. They often moved their belongings and families into improvised spaces within their lofts. As long as the building inspectors were busy other places, it was all right. However, as SoHo was discovered and chic little restaurants began to replace the cooperative kitchens, many artists were forced to vacate their spaces.

It was not long before the uptown art galleries saw the advantage of the much less expensive downtown locations for a second space. Today SoHo is honeycombed with expensive watering holes, trendy galleries and fancy shops. Many of the remaining artists in residence have been discovered and are commanding incredible prices for their work. The starving artists moved over to East Village, which is now slowly being gentrified.

On **Greene St.** you will see the longest continuous row of cast ⑤ iron buildings in the city. Turn left on Greene St. to the great cast iron building known as the **Queen of Greene Street at** Number 28-30 with its mansard roof, architectural details and bright blue paint.

Turn back and walk north on **Greene St.** Between Grand and Broome Sts. notice **Numbers 44** and **46-47 Greene St.** They are masonry structures with cast-iron ornamentation, including fancy scrollwork and medallions. At the southwest corner of Greene and Broome, notice the **Gunther Building at** Number 469-475 Broome St. with its curved panes of glass.

One block to your right at the corner of Broome and Broadway is one of the first of the cast irons, the **Haughwout Building,** ⑥ built in 1856, resembling a Venetian palace, now very blackened. This was the first building to use Otis's steam-powered passenger elevator.

Retrace your steps to **Greene St.** and turn right to 66 Greene St, once a store for the Lorillard tobacco company. The **King of Greene St.** is at Numbers 72-76. It is really two buildings, designed as one.

Then on to **West Broadway** with its shops and art galleries. Walk either north or south to explore this busy and exciting street.

Evening

Aфter all this walking, I suggest an early supper in Greenwich Village, an Off Broadway play in one of the village's many little theaters, and a nightcap at one of the famous jazz clubs.

Walk north to **Houston St**. and hail a cab. You can sometimes get a cab in the middle of Soho, but almost always on Houston St.

Ye Waverly Inn is at 16 Bank St. at Greenwich Ave. I would describe it as charmingly run-down Colonial American, with fireplaces and a nice outdoor garden in the summer. Best of all it is inexpensive. The chicken pot pie is great. Open for dinner from 5:15 to 10 p.m. No reservations are necessary, but if you would feel better, call.

Ray's Pizza at the corner of Sixth Ave. and 11th St. is considered one of the best pizza restaurants in New York. If you have some energy left, you may want to just get a slice of pizza and walk around the neighborhood. There are a few tables in the back next to the big Italian mural; most people stand at the chest-high counters to eat or just spill out onto the street.

After the theater, try one of the great jazz clubs such as the 52-year-old **Village Vanguard,** world-famous basement club at 178 Seventh Ave. between 11th and Perry Sts. Show times seven days a week 9:30 p.m., 11:30 p.m., and 1 a.m. Cover charge. Or try the **Blue Note** at 131 W. 3rd St. Show times are 9 and 11:30 p.m. with extra shows at 1:30 a.m. most nights. Open seven days a week 7 p.m. to 4 a.m. Music charge varies according to the artist. Or, **Sweet Basil**, at 88 7th Ave., with three shows nightly. By this point, if you are not exhausted, you are a New Yorker.

Day 3

Highlights: **Rockefeller Center, St. Patrick's Cathedral, Museum of Modern Art, Fifth Avenue stores, Bloomingdale's, Metropolitan Museum of Art.**

Reservations: **Cafe Des Artistes**, 1 W. 67th St., telephone 877-3500 or **Tavern on the Green**, Central Park at W. 67th St., telephone 873-3200.

Order tickets for a performance at **Lincoln Center** (theater, dance, concert or film). Buy tokens at a subway stop for the bus rides suggested in this tour.

Morning

If there is a center of Manhattan, it is probably at **Rockefeller Center** in midtown New York at 50th St. and Fifth Ave. Start your day here about 10 a.m. Rockefeller Center is a small city set in the middle of this large city. It was originally conceived as a home for the Metropolitan Opera, but between 1932 and 1940 it was converted into this extraordinary complex of buildings, gardens, shops, theaters and commerce.

As you walk down the Channel gardens, just off Fifth Ave., you will be facing **30 Rockefeller Plaza** with the British and French buildings on either side of you. The 70-story RCA Building faces a sunken plaza with a garden in the summer and a skating rink in the winter. A private street runs in front of the building. It is used by the public except for one day each year, when it is closed off to public traffic in order to maintain the right of ownership.

The gardens, which run from Fifth Ave. to the plaza, are planted and re-planted many times during the year to reflect the seasons. On occasion the gardens contain wonderful trees, pruned to represent exotic animals. At Christmas, huge white-and-gold angels play their musical instruments amid the Christmas plantings.

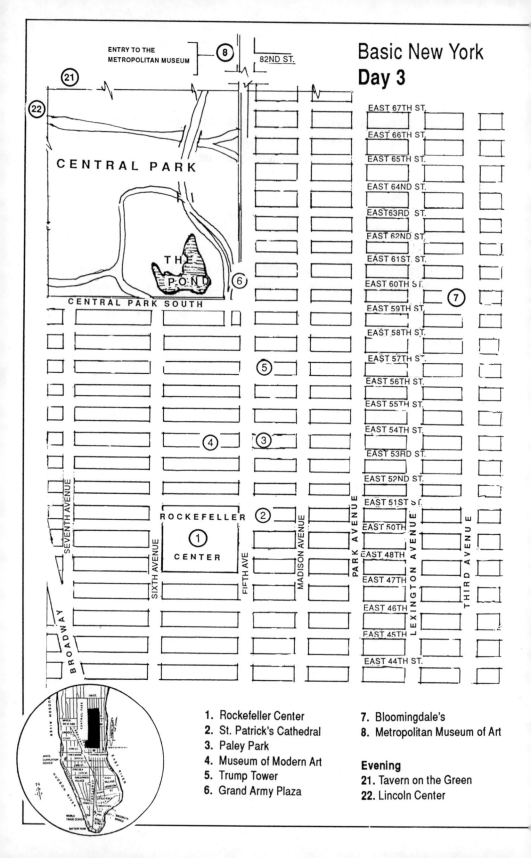

Basic New York
Day 3

1. Rockefeller Center
2. St. Patrick's Cathedral
3. Paley Park
4. Museum of Modern Art
5. Trump Tower
6. Grand Army Plaza
7. Bloomingdale's
8. Metropolitan Museum of Art

Evening
21. Tavern on the Green
22. Lincoln Center

Return to **Fifth Ave**. Across from Rockefeller Center is **St. Patrick's Cathedral**, the 11th largest in the world. As you walk through, notice the great canopied altar and fine stained glass. The third chapel on your right, as you face the altar, is very modern and stylized, dedicated to St. Elizabeth Seton, the first American born (United States) saint. ②

Walk north on Fifth Ave., past the banks, airline offices, book stores and jewelry shops to **53rd Avenue**. Step right a few paces on 53rd, to see the vest pocket **Paley Park** with its wall of water, tables and chairs and a counter for coffee or juice. It is a lovely oasis in this part of town. ③

On 53rd, on your left, is **St. Thomas' Church** (Episcopal). This is my favorite church in New York. Take a few minutes to run in to see the stained glass and magnificent altar screen. Every time I see this altar piece, with the sunlight streaming through sapphire blue windows behind the white screen with its figures of saints, martyrs and apostles, I feel the quick tears come. If you are lucky, someone may be practicing on the fine organ.

It should be about 11:30 a.m. Further west on 53rd St. is the **Museum of Modern Art,** one of the world's greatest collections. You have just time to visit the sculpture garden and Monet's water lily paintings on your quick visit today. ④

The sculpture garden is on the first floor; its Rodin, Renoir, and Picasso treasures are more than worth your time. You do not have time to see the collection — that is for another visit in the Art Lover's New York Chapter — but do take the escalator to the second floor, turn to your left to the room containing the Monet Waterlily paintings. It is quite special to be completely surrounded by these lovely images, like sinking in refreshing water.

Walk back to **Fifth Ave.** to continue your trek up this remarkable street. The stores get lusher and more expensive.

Walk the next few blocks on the east side of Fifth Ave. past Gucci, Elizabeth Arden with its red door and doorman, Bijan's where you have to make an appointment to buy anything, and Steuben glass at the corner of 56th St.

(5) Next comes the **Trump Tower.** You probably cannot afford to buy anything in any of the wildly expensive shops on the first few floors, but walk in anyway. The doorman will officiate and you will enter the most incredibly marbled first floor. Some days a tuxedoed pianist will be playing at the grand piano. Walk to the center of the building, which soars six floors upward, where you will be facing a marble wall of cascading water to the pools and fountains below.

On your left is a coffee bar, where you can order a cup to take to one of the little tables in front of the wall of water; sit and enjoy all the luxury. It is worth the over-priced coffee.

Just beyond Trump Tower is the three-story **Tiffany's**, for jewelry, silver, watches and other extravagant purchases. The window displays are usually jewels in themselves. Feel free to walk around the store, buying or not. Strangely enough, this is one of the elegant stores in the city where the clerks are very helpful and kind.

On the west side of the street you can visit **Van Cleef and Arpels,** again for jewelry, and **Bergdorf Goodman,** for all kinds of elegant clothing. If you need your hair done (women) while you are in New York, the beauty salon on one of the upper floors of Bergdorf's is accommodating to people without appointments. It is pleasant and professional.

(6) You are about to arrive at **59th St.** and one of the grand open spaces in the city, the **Grand Army Plaza** with the **Plaza Hotel** on your left and the General Motors Building on your right. The General Motors Building has now become home for F.A.O. Schwartz, the great toy shop.

An entrance to **Central Park** is directly in front of you. Here is where you will find the famous horse and buggies. Negotiate a half-hour trip. The price at last glance was $34 for a half-hour.

The **Plaza** is one of the great and stylish hotels in this town. Most of you will remember that this was home to Eloise, but you may not know that F. Scott Fitzgerald and his Zelda were guests along with The Beatles and Teddy Roosevelt. Tea in the hotel's **Palm Court** may be as close as you can get to an English experience in New York; the Oak Bar is dark and inviting

Lunch

Walk back to 57th St. where you have a choice of a number of "theme" restaurants between 6th and 7th Avenues: The **Brooklyn Diner**, with excellent chicken soup and egg creams; the tried-and-true **Hard Rock Cafe**, with first-rate pulled pork or "Pig" sandwich, or **Planet Hollywood**, with all its costumes, props and fabulous deserts; or, finally, one of New York's famous delis.

The **Carnegie Deli** is at 854 Seventh Ave. at 55th St. Many people think this is the best deli in the city. Everyone has their favorite. Try the huge pastrami sandwich and the excellent cole slaw. Order one sandwich and share. They are huge. No reservations necessary.

Afternoon

After lunch, save your feet and your energy and take a cab the short distance to the famous **Bloomingdale's** Department Store at 59th St., between Lexington and Third Avs. ⑦

This may be a combination of the best theater and museum in town. You cannot come to New York without setting foot in this center of entertainment, glitz and retail. Just wander from one little shop to the next, listen to the music, taste the food of the month, and buy something.

Walk the two blocks west to **Madison** and head north. Walk as far as you want past the incredible shops, galleries and restaurants. When you are ready, hop a bus to 82nd St., walk one block west to Fifth Ave. and the **Metropolitan Museum of Art**. ⑧

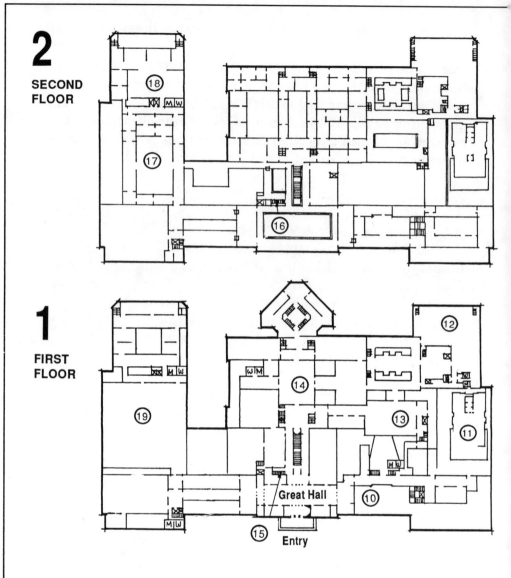

Metropolitan Museum of Art Floor Plan

First Floor

10. Egyptian Art
11. Temple of Dendur
12. The American Wing
13. Medieval Art
14. 16th-Century Spanish Patio
15. Escalator
19. African Art Galleries

Second Floor

16 Escalator
17. Impressionist/Post Impressionist Art
18. 20th-Century Art

Plan to be at the museum about 3:30 p.m. to allow about an hour and a half to see a few of the million objects in this collection. You understand that an hour in the Metropolitan is akin to attempting to empty the Atlantic Ocean with a teaspoon. Follow me on the shortest tour of the Met ever devised by a presumptuous guide.

Walk up the imposing front steps, into the **Great Hall.** Notice the magnificent bouquets in the four niches in the walls. They are always filled with glorious fresh flowers.

Admission is by paying a suggested donation, but it is more than a suggestion.

After you receive your little clip-on button, walk to the north end of the museum to the **Egyptian** galleries. If you are con- ⑩ fused, just ask at the information desk.

Walk through the galleries, just casually looking at some of the great masks, painted walls, and other artifacts until you arrive at the **Sackler Wing,** which houses the Temple of Dendur. It ⑪ was given to the United States as thanks for our contributions in saving the monuments submerged by the waters behind the Aswan Dam. The installation is very dramatic.

At the far end of the gallery, walk into the **American Wing,** ⑫ through the stained glass by Tiffany and Frank Lloyd Wright and the lovely courtyard. Walk to the room housing **Medieval** ⑬ **Art** for a look at the great 17th century choir screen from Valladolid, Spain and then through the Spanish patio galleries.

As you leave the Blumenthal patio, turn right and you will find ⑭ the escalator to the second floor.

When you step off the escalator, turn left and walk alongside ⑮ the great stairway. Turn left at the first doorway and follow the ⑯ signs to the **Impressionist and Post-Impressionist galleries,** filled with paintings by Renoir, Monet, Gauguin, Monet and van Gogh. Gallery 13 displays the museum's incredible collec- ⑰ tion of work by Edgar Degas.

(18) Just beyond these galleries are the **Twentieth Century Art Galleries,** a gift from Mrs. De Witt Wallace (of *Reader's Digest* fame).

Walk through one or two galleries on the second floor, take the stairway down to the main floor. You will walk through several more modern galleries on your way to the **Michael Rockefeller**
(19) **African Art Galleries**. Walk back to the Great Hall where you entered.

By now it should be getting on to 5:15 p.m. and closing time for the museum.

Evening

(20) Take a cab from in front of the museum to a restaurant near Lincoln Center. **Tavern on the Green** on West Central Park at 67th St. is spectacular with its mirrored walls, chandeliers and flowers. It is elegant and expensive. **Cafe Des Artistes** at 1 W. 67th St. between Central Park West and Columbus Ave. is beautiful and romantic and will be a bit less expensive than Tavern on the Green.

If you want something simpler and inexpensive, try the "**Lincoln Square Coffee Shoppe**", 2 Lincoln Square between 65th and 66th Sts., offering Viennese coffee, hamburgers, a very good salad bar and homemade pies. Or try the **Opera Espresso** at 1928 Broadway at 65th St., a nice coffee shop with good food and comfortable booths. Or on a nice evening, try **The Saloon** at Broadway at 64th St., across from Lincoln Center, with its great pizzas and outdoor seating.

Tonight go to a play, a concert, a dance performance or a movie
(21) at **Lincoln Center** on the upper west side of the city. This will give you a chance to wander around this remarkable space and see it illuminated. Be sure to notice the beautiful Chagall murals in the Metropolitan Opera foyer and the Henry Moore sculptures in the reflecting pool.

Three days in New York is almost a contradiction in terms, but perhaps now you have some sense of the size and diversity of this extraordinary city.

It is surprising how much you can see in a very few days. But there are always a few thousand places to visit on a return trip.

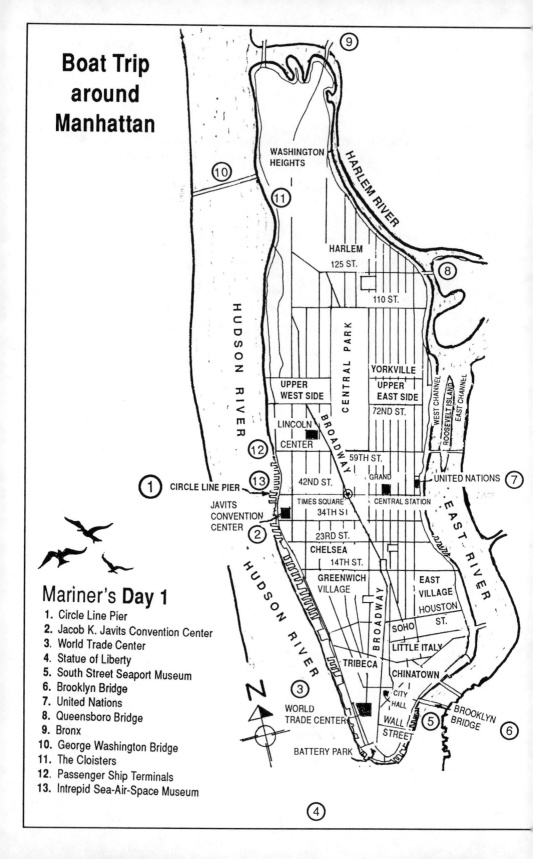

Boat Trip around Manhattan

Mariner's Day 1

1. Circle Line Pier
2. Jacob K. Javits Convention Center
3. World Trade Center
4. Statue of Liberty
5. South Street Seaport Museum
6. Brooklyn Bridge
7. United Nations
8. Queensboro Bridge
9. Bronx
10. George Washington Bridge
11. The Cloisters
12. Passenger Ship Terminals
13. Intrepid Sea-Air-Space Museum

Mariner's New York

Manhattan is mariner's territory. It is an island, a seaport, and it was the port of entry for millions of immigrants to the United States. To visit Mariner's New York is to visit New York.

Day 1

Highlights: Circle Line boat trip, the Intrepid Sea-Air-Space Museum, and the New York City Passenger Ship Terminal.

Reservations: Dinner on a restaurant-yacht, Spirit Cruises, Pier 62, foot of W. 23rd St. and Hudson River. *Telephone 727-2789.* Or World Yacht, Pier 81, W. 41st St. at Hudson River. *Telephone 630-8100.* Advance reservations are required. You must cancel within 48 hours or lose your money. Major credit cards accepted. Sails daily, year round, rain or shine. Heated in winter, air-conditioned in summer. Jackets required. Dinner cruise leaves at 7 p.m. and returns about 10 p.m. You can board an hour before sailing for cocktails or general sightseeing.

Suggestions: Binoculars are useful on the Circle Line boat trip. Also, remember, it is usually about 10 degrees cooler on the water, so dress accordingly.

Morning

(1) Start the day at **Pier 83** at the foot of West 42nd St. about 9:30 a.m. Here you will find the **Circle Line,** celebrating over 40 years of service as it plies the waters around Manhattan. This excellent sightseeing organization offers three-hour tours around the entire island. This is one of the finest ways a mariner, or anybody else, can spend a morning seeing the city from the water. Sailing times change with the calendar, but they usually begin about 9:30 a.m. and run every half hour during the summer months; less often in the spring and fall. Call 563-3200 or check the newspaper or tourist magazines to find out precise times. They do not operate in January or February.

There is a commentary aboard, which describes the highlights along the way, but let me supply a brief summary of the major sights you will see on this 35-mile trip. The boat sails south, (2) passing first, on your left, the **Jacob K. Javits Convention Center** covering 1.8 million square feet. Architect I. M. Pei designed the building with reflective glass to mirror the city during the day and with interior lighting to give the structure a translucent quality at night. The building is so large that the Statue of Liberty could fit inside the Crystal Palace lobby. It is ironic that this gorgeous new center was built next to the moldering old passenger piers. Plans are afoot to clean up and convert the piers to other uses. On your right is New Jersey with its equally ugly factories.

(3) The view improves rapidly as you pass the twin towers of the **World Trade Center,** the financial center buildings, and then (4) enter the harbor, where you will circle the **Statue of Liberty.** Notice the graceful **Verrazano Narrows Bridge,** linking Manhattan to Staten Island, just beyond the lady. You will pass Ellis Island and Governor's Island. As you circle around, you will enter the East River.

(5) On your left you will pass the **South Street Seaport,** with its collection of historic sailing ships, and travel under the great (6) **Brooklyn Bridge.**

You will pass beneath 20 bridges on this day's cruise.

Next come the **United Nations** buildings, followed by the roof-
top gardens in Sutton Place, an exclusive residential area. On
your right you will pass **Roosevelt Island**, now a residential
enclave, linked to Manhattan by an aerial tramway. Just opposite Roosevelt Island's lighthouse, on your left, you will see
Gracie Mansion, home of New York's mayor.

As you glide under the **Queensboro Bridge,** you will get a
glimpse of the East Harlem slums. At this point you will be
moving along the **Harlem River**, which joins the East River
with the Hudson at the northern point of the island. To the
north of you is the **Bronx**.

You are now at the northern edge of the island and ready to re-
enter the Hudson River. Look north to see the river as it widens
and flows alongside the Palisades (cliffs). You will sail under
the **George Washington Bridge** and past the **Cloisters,** the
Metropolitan Museum of Art's great medieval museum. South
on the Hudson River, you'll go past Grant's Tomb, the **pas-**
senger ship terminals and the aircraft carrier, *Intrepid*, and the
Intrepid Sea-Air-Space Museum, which you will visit this
afternoon.

And now you are back at your starting point.

Noon

Y ou should return to the pier about noon or 12:30 p.m., just
in time for lunch. Walk east a block or so to **Eleventh Ave.,**
turn left and walk north four short blocks to 46th St. **The**
Landmark Tavern is at 626 11th Ave. at 46th St. Open daily
from noon to midnight, it takes no reservations or credit cards.
It is an old (1868) waterfront tavern, recently remodeled. Stick
to the standard fare of fish and chips, hamburgers, shepherd's
pie and Irish soda bread, all of which they serve in their 19th
century rooms. A brunch is served on Saturday and Sunday
from noon to 4:30 p.m. 46th St. is called Restaurant Row, and
this tavern is the westernmost outpost of the line of chic eating

spots further east. I think you will like this place; I do.

Afternoon

After lunch at the tavern, walk west on 46th St. to the Hudson River and **Pier 86** at the foot of W. 46th St. to visit the **Intrepid Sea-Air-Space Museum**. The building of *Intrepid* was begun six days before the Japanese attack on Pearl Harbor, December 7, 1941. This Essex-class carrier has eleven decks above the main deck (plus the 64 foot mast) and seven more decks down into the hold. She recorded more than 100,000 aircraft landings during her 31-year career.

This World War II and Vietnam War aircraft carrier is a floating museum. A trip aboard will give you a look at the past, present and future of air, space and sea technology. You can explore real aircraft on the 900-foot flight deck and climb the control bridges.

There is an admission charge to go aboard the *Intrepid*. Children under six are admitted free as are military personnel. The museum is open Wednesday through Sunday, from 10 a.m. to 5 p.m. year round, seven days a week, May through Labor Day. Call 245-0072 to double check open hours.

There are a number of steps to negotiate from the dock to the first deck, plus an additional 45 steps to the flight deck. A third set of steps will take you to the bridge. You will board on the **Hangar Deck**. Here you will find Intrepid Hall, the Hall of Honor, Pioneers Hall, Technologies Hall, and the cafeteria and restrooms.

Technologies Halls displays let you travel from the bottom of the ocean to outer space. Pioneers Hall tells the history of our flying machines. A wide-screen movie recreates the experience of being on a flight deck as jets land and take off. A recreation of the Battle of Leyte Gulf, when the Intrepid itself was hit by four Japanese Kamikaze pilots, is presented in Intrepid Hall. It is awesome when you realize you are standing on the very decks set afire by these suicide missions. I was amazed at the size of the flight deck and the number of aircraft anchored in place. As you walk forward on the deck, you will be rewarded by a wonderful view of the Hudson and the far shore. Notice the Floating Hospital, which houses a free clinic, anchored at a nearby dock. The Gallery Deck, above the Hangar Deck, contains the Combat Information Center; the Flight Deck enables you to get a close look at *Intrepid's* air wing. Then you can climb up into the Island and tour her bridges. Below the Flight Deck you will find the Gallery Deck crew's quarters. Check for any other additions to this floating museum. Be sure to visit the excellent gift shop as you leave.

Next to the *Intrepid* is the **New York City Recreation Pier**, outfitted with benches, planters and sculpture. It is a fine spot to relax between sightseeing attractions.

The **New York City Passenger Ship Terminal** spreads along the Hudson River from 46th to 54th Sts. Opened in 1974, this modern terminal has three levels: the street level for supplies, the roof-top car park for vehicles and the middle level for passengers. Observation decks are open to the public without charge.

This is a port of call for the world's largest and most luxurious cruise ships, such as the *Queen Elizabeth II*, the *Scandinavia* and the *Royal Viking*. Check the newspapers to see which ships will be in port. Access to individual liners is reserved for passengers. Tight security now prevents sightseeing visits aboard anchored ships. However you can walk along the docks and take the escalators or elevators to the observation decks. It is a grand sight when these ships are in port.

Evening

If you have not had enough of ships for the day, plan dinner aboard one of the luxury yachts docking at **Pier 62**, West 23rd St., or Pier 8 at W. 41st St. on the Hudson River. Boats depart at 7 p.m. and return at 10 p.m. Dining is available inside or on the open deck, depending on the weather. This should be a fitting end to your first day in Mariner's New York.

Day 2

Highlights: The Battery, Castle Clinton, Admiral George Dewey Promenade, the Statue of Liberty, Ellis Island and an evening sail on the yacht *Petrel*. Statue of Liberty Information for the ferry, *telephone 269-5755*.

Reservations: Evening sail on the yacht *Petrel*, Battery Park. Reservations and prepaid tickets necessary. *Call 825-1976*. No refunds or date transfers. The ship sails, rain or shine.

Clothing recommendations: Dress casually and comfortably for this day of walking, boating and sailing. No hard-soled shoes are allowed on the yacht's teak decks. Remember it is usually about 10 degrees cooler on the water than on land, so bring a jacket or sweater. You might want to consider bringing binoculars.

Morning

① Start the day at 9:30 a.m. at **Bowling Green** on the south end of the island, known as **The Battery**. You can cab, bus or take the Lexington Ave. I.R.T. subway.

Whether or not you take the subway, take a minute to notice the entrance/exit kiosk, the only one remaining from early subway construction. This Beaux-Arts building is part of the Bowling Green renovation.

Captain Adrianen Block and his crew of the ill-fated *Tiger* landed here in 1613, only to be forced to remain when their ship burned to the waterline. They survived to build another ship and sailed into Long Island Sound to discover Block Island, named for the captain.

Here, near the Green, the first Dutch settlers built their mud homes in 1625. In 1733, Bowling Green became the city's first official park. It was the site of demonstrations during the American Revolution, including the destruction of a statue of George III once located here.

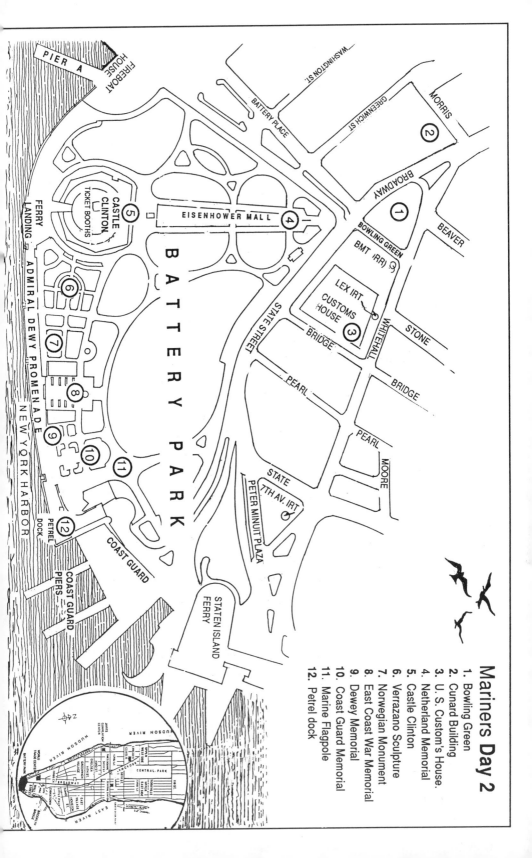

Mariners Day 2

1. Bowling Green
2. Cunard Building
3. U. S. Custom's House.
4. Netherland Memorial
5. Castle Clinton
6. Verrazano Sculpture
7. Norwegian Monument
8. East Coast War Memorial
9. Dewey Memorial
10. Coast Guard Memorial
11. Marine Flagpole
12. Petrel dock

(2) Across from Bowling Green, at 25 Broadway, is the old **Cunard Building,** now a post office. Take a minute to step into what was once the finest interior of any building in the city. It is still extraordinary, despite the dreadful renovation by the postal service. Once the home of the great steamship line, Cunard, the space reflects the elegance and romance of the period. Notice the great dome with beautiful ceiling designs, the arched entrances, second story colonnades and the frescoes of ships captained by Leif Ericson, Columbus, Sir Francis Drake and John Cabot. Maps of the world steamship routes are on the north and south walls.

Just south of Bowling Green is what used to be the **United States Custom House** for the port of New York. Designed by (3) Cass Gilbert, this Beaux-Arts building has an extraordinary facade. A double row of statues top the huge columns while a lower group of sculptures symbolizes the continents: Asia, Europe, the Americas and Africa. This is now the home of the Smithsonian's Museum of the American Indian; Customs Offices have been moved to the World Trade Center.

As you begin your walk through **Battery Park,** notice the huge granite flagstaff honoring the first Dutch settlers, the **Nether-** (4) **lands Memorial**.

As you walk south on the **Eisenhower Mall,** you will see the sculpture of John Ericsson, inventor of the iron-clad Civil War battleship *Monitor*, on your right. At the foot of the mall is the bronze sculpture of *The Immigrants*, honoring the millions who passed through Castle Clinton.

(5) The entrance to **Castle Clinton National Monument** is in front of you. It is now a visitor's center and the place to buy tickets for your ferry ride to the **Statue of Liberty** and **Ellis Island** this morning. The ferry operates seven days a week. A single adult ticket is $7; $5 for seniors, and $3 for children, 3 to 17 years. Ferries leave from 9:30 a.m. to 3:30 p.m. in the winter and from 9 a.m. to 5 p.m. in the summer for this 15-minute trip.

The fare for the ferry entitles you to go to both the Statue of

Liberty and Ellis Island. The ferry shuttles back and forth between the two islands, free of charge.

Be warned. Since the renovation, the Statue of Liberty and Ellis Island have become the city's *number one* tourist attractions.There are long lines in the summer, particularly on weekends, for the ferry and to take the elevator to the top of Miss Liberty's pedestal.

Castle Clinton is open, free, from 9 a.m. to 5 p.m. daily during the summer; Monday to Friday from September to December. This was the original fort on the Battery. Built in 1807, its circular 8-foot-thick walls and 28 cannons were one of the island's major defenses. Later it served as a concert hall where P.T. Barnum's Jenny Lind sang, and in 1855 it was opened as an immigrant landing station prior to Ellis Island's opening in 1892. It served as the city Aquarium until 1941. It was almost demolished, but saved at the last minute, renovated in time for the Bicentennial, and currently houses a small exhibition space.

Buy your tickets, then walk along the shoreline on the **Admiral George Dewey Memorial Promenade** to enjoy the view of the harbor, the Statue of Liberty, and Ellis Island. Notice the **Fireboat** station on **Pier A** and the clock tower commemorating servicemen who died in World War I. The clock rings ships' bells each hour.

The lines for the **ferry** will greet you as you walk along the promenade. When you board the ferry, you can choose to sit either on the lower, enclosed decks or on the open top decks. I always choose the top decks where you can see the beautiful views of Manhattan from the water, as well as watch the lady move toward you.

Noon

After landing on **Liberty Island,** you may want to stop at the restaurant, immediately to your right as you leave the dock. A cafeteria is located inside the building and on nice days, which is the only kind of day you should come here, outdoor seating is adjacent to the restaurant. The service is slow and the food is average New York street food, but the prices are low and the ambience and views are superb. Notice the silver wrought-iron furniture with intricate designs of acorns and oak leaves. Relax under the shady trees, with the Verrazano Bridge in the distance and the Lady looming overhead. Eat your hamburgers and feed your crumbs to the greedy sea gulls. I love sitting here.

Afternoon

There are several ways to see the statue. Waiting two to three hours to make the 22-story climb to the crown of the statue is not on my list. Nor is the long wait to take the elevator to the top of the pedestal. We tried that on our last visit. Unfortunately, you are so close to the base of the pedestal that you have no perspective on the lady; all I could see were her toes.

I think the best way to get the closest, and still be able to see the statue, is to walk up to the third level, a comfortable climb, and stroll out on the promenade where you are some distance from the lady. You will also have excellent views of the harbor and the city skyline. The **Immigration Exhibit** is also located on the third level; the Statue of Liberty exhibition is on the second level. Both are worth your time. Be sure to notice the old torch on display on the ground floor. One final tip: the restrooms are on the balcony level.

Take the free ferry to **Ellis Island.** As you approach the island, the newly renovated Ellis Island Immigration Museum almost looks like a great resort hotel with its four great towers, arches and stone and red brick facade.

Before going into the building, take a walk along the 971-foot sea wall, with its 470 copper panels with the names of families who passed through Ellis Island. You can also see the fabulous view of Manhattan Island and Lady Liberty.

The designers of the museum should be congratulated as much on what they did not do as what they did. As you walk into the great baggage room, all you will see are a small information desk to the side and carts filled with some of the original baggage carried into this place by early immigrants. You must populate this space with the people in your imagination. Take the time to watch the half-hour theater production "Island of Hope/Island of Tears, which covers the Ellis Island years from 1892 to 1924. It will be a great help as you visit the rest of the museum.

Take the steps or the elevator to the upstairs **Registry Room** where immigrants were processed and received medial examinations. Again the room has been left bare except for the small lines of benches. A catwalk will take you on a walk around the room.

Among the many rooms of exhibitions I would recommend in particular visiting the rooms which contain "Treasures from Home." These are filled with objects actually brought to this country by immigrants and donated to the museum.

You can spend hours here or on a short visit like this one, see the film, visit the two great open spaces, the Registry and Baggage rooms, and look at "Treasures from Home." Plan to come back. A pleasant cafeteria with a large selection of ethnic food and beers and a very complete shop are located on the first floor.

Plan to return to shore in time for a 5:30 p.m. **sail** aboard the 70-foot yacht, the *Petrel*, or if you prefer, take the 7:30 p.m. sunset sail, Monday and Friday only. If you want a quick bite to eat, there are stands such as Nathan's Famous, selling Coney Island red hots and other such nourishing delicacies.

When you disembark from the ferry, walk east on the **Promenade,** to your right as you step off the gangplank. Look to your far left to see the **Verrazzano sculpture,** honoring the ⑥ Italian explorer who sailed into New York Harbor in 1524. The **Norwegian Maritime Monument** honoring the Norwegian ⑦ Merchant Marines who served during World War II is next on your left.

⑧ You then arrive at the enormous **East Coast War Memorial** with its huge eagle and four large honor rolls paying tribute to members of the Armed Forces lost in the Atlantic during World ⑨ War II. Continue past the **Admiral George Dewey Memorial** honoring the hero of the Spanish American War and the bronze ⑩ **Coast Guard Memorial** in memory of the men and women of the Coast Guard who served in World War II.

⑪ Behind the Coast Guard Memorial is the **Marine Flagpole**, a large ship's mast symbolizing Battery Park's marine significance; it stands 102 feet high.

By now you will have reached the end of the **Promenade**. The ⑫ **Petrel Dock** is next to the U.S. Coast Guard buildings. You may have to search for the tiny little house which serves as its office. Designed by Sparkman & Stephens and built in New York in 1938, she was once owned by the U.S. Coast Guard Academy. The *Petrel* developed an impressive ocean racing record and was a favorite of the late President John F. Kennedy, who sailed her often. She weighs 32 tons and carries up to 3,000 square feet of sail on her 90-foot mainmast and 40-foot mizzen.

She sails from mid-April to the middle of September for lunch, happy hour, sunset and moonlight sails. Prepaid reservations are usually necessary; there are no refunds or date transfers. Call the *Petrel* office at 825-1976 for updated information on sailing times and prices. There are usually additional trips on weekends.

The yacht sails rain or shine subject to cancellation only at the captain's discretion. There is a bar aboard; passengers cannot carry their own beverages nor are they allowed to bring radios with them. Remember, it is much cooler on the water so dress appropriately. Wear sneakers or other soft-soled shoes; no hard soles are allowed on the teak decks. You can just relax and sip your drink, or you can help raise the mainsail. You will come back refreshed. As they say, sailing is man in harmony with the elements.

Evening

Since you are not dressed up, I suggest that after your sail, you try a restaurant which is not dressed up. Grab a cab, usually very easy to get in that part of town, and go up to the **Bridge Cafe,** 279 Water St. at Dover St., on the edge of the South Street Seaport, where you will spend the day tomorrow. This is a very unpretentious 19th-century saloon with excellent food, particularly good seafood, and reasonable prices. It serves dinner until midnight, but only until 11 p.m. on Sundays. No reservations and no credit cards.

The last time I was there the menu included such wonderful items as saffron mussel soup; warmed oysters with fennel; spinach and pernod; and sauteed shrimp with tomato and crab sauce. And, yes, they do serve other entrees besides fish. On that same menu were roast duck with a green peppercorn sauce; escallops of veal with fried ginger and white wine; and stuffed breast of chicken with brandied black peppercorns, lemon and fresh herbs. Entrees are moderate in price.

Tomorrow you will explore the environs of the Bridge Cafe. For tonight, just enjoy the good food and relaxed atmosphere of this funky neighborhood treasure.

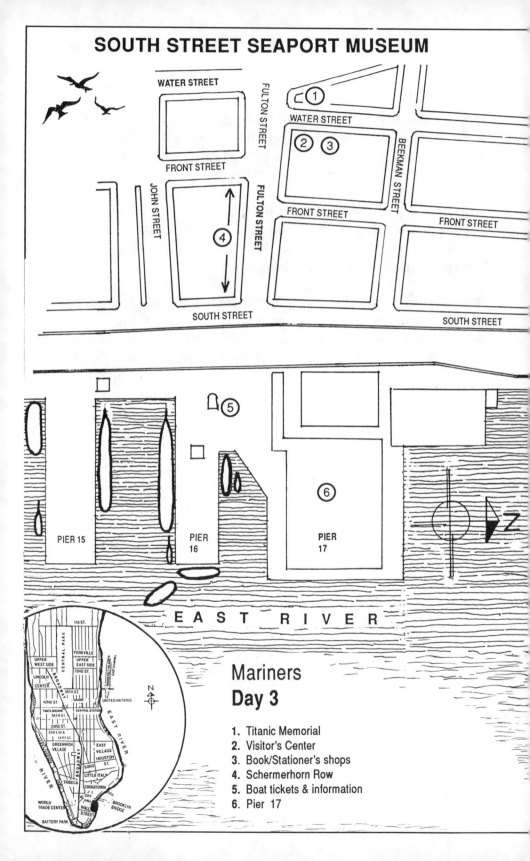

SOUTH STREET SEAPORT MUSEUM

WATER STREET

FULTON STREET

WATER STREET

FRONT STREET

BEEKMAN STREET

JOHN STREET

FULTON STREET

FRONT STREET

FRONT STREET

SOUTH STREET

SOUTH STREET

PIER 15

PIER 16

PIER 17

EAST RIVER

Mariners
Day 3

1. Titanic Memorial
2. Visitor's Center
3. Book/Stationer's shops
4. Schermerhorn Row
5. Boat tickets & information
6. Pier 17

Day 3

Highlights: South Street Seaport Museum.

Reservations: Sailing on schooner *Pioneer*, South Street Seaport, Telephone 669-9400.

Clothing recommendations: Wear comfortable clothing, soft-soled shoes for walking and sailing. No high heels or hard soled shoes are allowed on the schooner. Remember it is cooler on the water than on land, so dress appropriately.

Dinner: Liberty Cafe and Oyster Bar, Pier 17. South Street Seaport. *Telephone 406-1111.*

Membership suggestion: Free admission is just one of the benefits of membership in South Street Seaport Museum. It includes reduced rates for Pioneer sails, discounts in the shops, a magazine and invitations to special events. For information write: Membership Department, South Street Seaport Museum, 207 Front Street, New York, N.Y. 10038. *Telephone 748-8766.* The most recent brochure lists Individual memberships at $35; Student and Senior citizen memberships at $25 and Family memberships at $50.

Morning

You are going to spend today in the 33-acre site designated as the **South Street Seaport Museum**. Take a cab to the seaport. If your driver wants more of an address, tell him to drop you at the corner of Fulton and Water Sts., a good starting point for your day's exploration. The piers, shops, ships and galleries open at 11 a.m.; most remain open until 6 p.m. Many of the shops stay open till 9 p.m. and the restaurants are open till midnight and beyond.

This eleven-block district was the center of New York's 19th-century port. From here the ferries crossed to Brooklyn as early as 1816. The **Fulton Produce Market** opened in 1822; it later became a fish market. But it was the opening of the Erie Canal in

1825 which established this as the major port in the United States as goods from the Midwest poured into New York for export.

In the 1860s, as sail ships made room for steamships, the port declined. The steamships moved to the deep-water piers on the Hudson River. The area continued to wane until the mid-1960s when a group of concerned citizens began work to save the old port. The renovation of old buildings and sailing ships along with the development of new commercial spaces has turned this area into one of the most exciting sections of the city.

(1) The **Titanic Memorial Tower** is located at the entrance to the Seaport, at the corner of Fulton and Water Sts. The tower is in memory of those who perished on the ocean liner *Titanic*, lost on her maiden voyage in 1912.

(2) Just beyond, at 207 Water St., is the **Museum Visitors' Center**. This building and the adjacent ones represent the classic New York waterfront and commercial architecture of the first half of the 19th-century. Built in 1835-36, they are in the Greek Revival Style. Note the brick facade, granite steps and post and lintel storefronts.

(3) Next to the Visitors' Center is **Browne & Company Stationers** where you can watch letterpress printing and buy fine hand-printed stationery. Just beyond is the book and chart store with an incredible selection of maps, books and other publications about boats, sails, navigation and all subjects dear to a sailor's heart.

(4) Walk over to Fulton St., turn left toward the river, past the seaport's architectural jewel, **Schermerhorn Row**, 2-20 Fulton St., the preserved warehouses and counting houses of the original port. Note particularly the pitched roofs, plus the mansard roof at Numbers 2-4, added for extra room when a hotel was located there.

Noon

The *Pioneer* is the only ship at the Seaport operating under sail. Built in 1885, she worked as a sloop with one mast carrying sand for iron making on the Delaware River, then as a schooner with two masts and finally as a power-driven oil tanker with both masts removed. She was donated to the museum in 1970. Cruises leave Pier 16 at the end of Fulton St. on South St. several times a day from May to September. Reservations are encouraged.Call 748-8786, 9:30 a.m. to 5:30 p.m., to check sailing times, prices and to make reservations. The course depends on wind and tides. You may bring food and drink aboard, but you must wear soft-soled shoes. Maximum, 25 passengers.

If you want to stay ashore, explore **Pier 17**, the newest building ⑥ at the seaport, standing on the site of the fish market's old piers. Its glass-enclosed exterior and open decks look like a giant ship about to set sail. Escalate up to the third floor and promenade for food, but first walk out on the open decks overlooking the East River to see the view. Consider bringing your food out on this deck and sitting on one of the reclining deck chairs. It really feels like a short trip on an ocean liner as you lounge, eat and watch the river traffic sail past.

Inside, you have a choice of a dozen different food bars. Try a moveable feast: one-half dozen oysters, about $6, from the Liberty Oyster Bar, a salad from Salad Mania and dessert from an ice cream shop. Or you can have Mexican, Oriental, a slice of pizza at Pizza on the Pier or a Coney Island at Hot Dog.

Afternoon

After lunch you will want to explore some of the historic ships anchored at the seaport. The South Street Seaport Museum's pierside information center was originally the pilothouse of the steam tugboat *New York Central No. 31*. Check ⑤ at the center for information about which ships are available for exploration.

The four-masted *Peking*, 347 feet, built in Germany in 1911, carried more than an acre of sail. She moved general cargo from Europe to the west coast of South America and returned with nitrates to fertilize the fields of Europe. In 1931, she became a training ship at a British boys' school and remained there until she was purchased by the museum in 1974. The *Ambrose Lightship*, 1908, 135 feet, escorted ships through the Ambrose Channel into New York harbor for more than 20 years. She was the Seaport's first ship.

The full-rigged ship *Wavertree*, 1885, 293 feet, is the largest iron-hulled sailing vessel currently preserved in a museum. This British ship, descendent of the 19th-century clipper ships, transported jute from Bangladesh to Britain, rounding the Cape of Good Hope on both legs of the voyage. Following a storm off Cape Horn in 1910, when she was dismasted, she served as a floating warehouse in the Straits of Magellan for 37 years. In 1966 she was discovered and found to be in good condition. She was towed to the Seaport where her decks were rebuilt, her masts restored and her living quarters and the rest of her rigging renovated.

The *Lettie G. Howard*, 1893, 74 feet, is a wooden fishing schooner built in Essex, Massachusetts. Early in the century, the Fulton Fish Market was crowded with such schooners, unloading fish and loading salt for their return to Cape Cod and Nova Scotia. Onboard is an exhibition about the life on these schooners in those early years.

At the far end of the piers is the **Ship Model Shop and Craft Center** where sometimes you can see the wood carvers working. Commissions for models are accepted.

After your busy afternoon, wander up to the third level of **Pier 17**, order a drink or coffee from one of the many vendors and sit out on the deck to relax and watch the river traffic and the tall ships you have just visited.

Evening

Plan to eat supper in the Seaport area this evening. There are a dozen or more good restaurants. **Sloppy Louie's** and **Sweet's** are the old seaport restaurants where many tourists go to eat fish and enjoy the atmosphere. I like the **Liberty Cafe** at Pier 17 with its great views, good food and moderate prices. They serve daily until midnight.

In three short days you have explored the port city of New York, sailed her ships, traveled her ferries, boarded her museum boats and eaten from the bounty of her nearby waters. You have reminded yourself of New York's great maritime past and perhaps better understand America's connection to the sea.

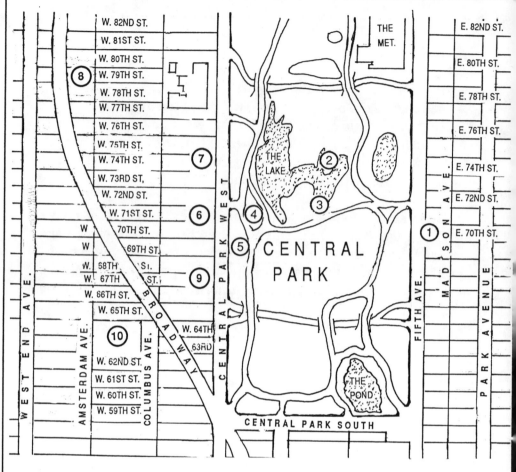

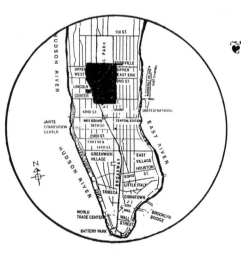

Romantic **D A Y 1**

1. Frick Collection
2. The Lake & Loeb Boathouse
3. Bethesda Fountain
4. Strawberry Fields
5. Tavern on the Green
6. Dakota Apartments
7. San Remo Apartments
8. Hayden Planetarium
9. Zabar's store
10. Cafe des Artistes
11. Lincoln Center

Romantic New York

For travelers with romance in their souls, no place provides more spots for hand-holding, dallying and strolling than Manhattan. Secluded parks, pretty restaurants, gorgeous views, horse-drawn carriages, and gondola rides provide the most romantic settings in the world. The walks in this chapter take you to some of the loveliest and most charming parts of the city: down old streets in Greenwich Village, on a cable car ride and on pathways along the river. It is possible to find tranquil, secluded spots in the middle of all the hurly-burly of this enormous city.

❦ Day 1

Highlights: Frick Collection, a boat ride and **lunch in Central Park**, a walk in a **historic district, Zabar's Delicatessen,** and music at **Lincoln Center**.

Reservations: Reserve a rowboat or space in a gondola in Central Park. *Telephone 517-2233.*

Lunch at Tavern on the Green. Central Park W. and 67th St. *Telephone 873-3200.* Or The Boathouse Cafe. Central Park. *Telephone 517-2233.*

Dinner at **Cafe Des Artistes. 1** W. 67th St. (Jackets and ties required for men) *Telephone 877-3500.*

Tickets for a performance at Lincoln Center.

Morning

① **A**cross from Central Park on Fifth Ave. at 70th St. is the most romantic museum in New York, the **Frick Collection**. It opens at 10 a.m. Here you will find beautiful paintings by the romantic artists, gorgeous French furniture, lush carpets, and elegant draperies. This is a manageable museum: you can walk through it easily in an hour. Needless to say, you could spend much more time, but an hour's stay can be enormously rewarding. It is open Tuesday through Saturday, 10 a.m. to 6 p.m., Sunday, 1 to 6 p.m. Closed Monday. Admission. Incidentally, visitors under age 16 are not admitted without an adult. Children under 10 are not admitted at all.

The steel magnate, Henry Clay Frick, built both the collection and the house. Originally planned for Pittsburgh, Frick changed his mind and settled for New York. He was concerned that the pollution from his steel mills would affect the collection. The house was opened to the public in 1935.

A small anteroom is on your right where you can check your coat and packages. The great **Boucher Room** is on your left as you enter the main section of the house. If you had to pick the most romantic of all painters, it would probably be Boucher or Fragonard; the Fragonards are just beyond. Notice the elegant draperies, carpet and period furniture.

Walk through the **dining room** with its English portraits by Gainsborough, Hogarth and Romney, and enter the **Fragonard Room** with its large panels depicting The Progress of Love. Note the Sevres vase in the shape of a ship and the tapestry-covered armchairs.

The **living room** contains some of the greatest paintings in the collection: Titian's *Portrait of a Man in a Red Cap* and the fat old

Pietro Aretino; Bellini's *St. Francis* and El Greco's *St. Jerome*. Again note the furniture by the master Boulle.

Pass through the **library** with its 18th-century English portraits and Renaissance bronzes to the West Gallery. Notice particularly Rembrandt's Polish Rider and his Self-Portrait; Goya's *The Forge* and Hals' *Portrait of an Elderly Man*.

Next is the **Enamel Room**, the smallest room in the museum, with Frick's own collection of painted French enamels from the workshops at Limoges. The **Oval Room** at the other end of the West Gallery contains a wonderful terracotta *Diana the Huntress* by Houdon.

Time to sit for a few minutes in the **Garden Court** and enjoy the plantings and fountains and portrait busts.

Just off the court, take time to walk through the **North Hall** to see Monet's *Vetheuil in Winter* and Ingres's *Comtesse d'-Haussonville*. The **South Hall**, on your way to the entrance hall, is filled with lovely paintings by Boucher, Corot and an especially wonderful Vermeer, *Officer and Laughing Girl*. Note the desk made for Marie Antoinette by Riesener. Renoir's *Mother and Children* is at the end of this hall on your right. It is very easy to miss, but worth the few extra steps.

Walk back to **Fifth Ave.**, turn right and continue two blocks to 72nd St. Cross Fifth Ave. and enter **Central Park**. Turn right at the next major pathway, East Drive, and continue to **The Lake** and the **Loeb Boathouse**. Time for a leisurely excursion. Call 517-2233 to make reservations for a ride in the **Venetian gondola** or to rent a row boat. Call 861-4137 to reserve a bike and for information about deposits and necessary identification.

Noon

By now it should be about noon and time for lunch. If you are in New York in good weather, plan to eat your lunch right here at the **Boat House Cafe**. This is a lovely, sit-down restaurant, overlooking the lake and boat traffic. The ambience is wonderful, the food and service are good and the prices are moderate. And now is the time for your boat ride on New York's only gondola.

If the weather is not so nice, plan a later lunch on the other side of the park at **Tavern on the Green**. In either event the following walk is the same.

Retrace your steps to the 72nd St. Transverse, turn right at the
(3) **Trefoil Arch** and continue to the **Bethesda Fountain and Terrace**. Look over the parapet to see the fountain with its statue, Angel of the Waters, and its four cherubs representing Temperance, Purity, Health and Peace.

(4) Continue west to **Strawberry Fields**, named in honor of John Lennon, songwriter and singer, and made possible by his widow, Yoko Ono. The name comes from one of his popular songs, *Strawberry Fields Forever*. This is one of the loveliest and most romantic gardens in the park.

Walk south on the main path from the fields until you arrive at
(5) **Tavern on the Green**, where you will be surrounded by trees filled with twinkling lights. Many folks think this is a tourist trap. Well, if it is, let me be trapped. I love it. Where else can you eat in a huge glassed-in restaurant filled with Baccarat chandeliers, multi-colored ceiling and other splendors, all in the middle of one of the world's greatest parks? Mirrors, flowers and elegant table appointments complete this magical place. Actually there are six different dining rooms which provide service daily, from noon until midnight. It is not inexpensive, but the ambience and food are worth every cent. Don't ignore their desserts.

Afternoon

(6) After a leisurely lunch, exit the park at 72nd St. Just across West Central Park are the **Dakota apartments**, home of the late John Lennon. When the Dakota was built in 1884, it was so far "out of town" that someone said it might as well be in the Dakota territory. Edward S. Clark, heir to the Singer Sewing

machine fortune and builder of the Dakota, liked the idea so much that he asked the architect to include some details from the Far West. Notice the ears of corn and arrowheads worked into the design and the Indian head above the gate. The Dakota was the setting for the horror movie, Rosemary's Baby.

Walk north, past Numbers 145-146 Central Park West, the **San** ⑦ **Remo Apartments**, between W. 74th and 75th Sts. Note the twin towers, capped with Roman temples and finials.

Continue north to 76th St., turn left and walk a block or two down the tree-lined sidewalk. This is one of New York's loveliest historic districts. Walk back to **Central Park West** on 77th St. and turn left. Many of the streets along here, just west of West Central Park, are filled with row housing built at the turn of the century. They represent some of the most romantic styles: neo-Baroque, Italian Renaissance, and Roman Revival.

Walk three blocks west on 80th St. to 2245 Broadway at 80th to visit **Zabars**, one of the world's great food bazaars. Open 365 ⑧ days a year, Monday through Friday, 8 a.m. to 7:30 p.m., Saturday to midnight; Sunday to 6 p.m. In addition to all the fabulous food: imported cheeses and coffee, smoked fish, fresh caviar, breads, and pasta, it also sells cookware and appliances. Prices are usually very competitive. Tucked in the back of the store is **Delices Guy Pascal**, serving coffee and French pastries.

Evening

Perhaps the most romantic restaurant in New York is **Cafe des Artistes** at 1 W. 67th St. Take a cab or a Central Park West bus south to 67th St. The restaurant is located in the lobby of the **Hotel des Artistes**, a building designed specifically for ⑨ artists. Noel Coward, Isadora Duncan and Norman Rockwell all called this home. The restaurant is decorated with 1917 murals of female nudes by Howard Chandler Christy and leaded glass windows. The country French cuisine and service are elegant, as befits a place which requires reservations, and jackets and ties for its male guests.

After dinner, walk three blocks south on West Central Park to 64th St., turn right one block and you will be facing Lincoln Center, where you will be attending a concert tonight.

(10) The sight of **Lincoln Center**, lit at night, may be one of the loveliest views in town. Home of the **Metropolitan Opera, New York City Opera and Ballet**, the **New York Philharmonic, Julliard School of Music, Avery Fisher Hall** and several magnificent theatres, this center is surrounded by plazas, fountains, pools, sculptures and tree-filled walkways. Through the glass facade of the opera house, you can see the huge Chagall paintings which form the backdrop for the lobby.

With luck, you can end your first romantic day with a *Mostly Mozart* concert or something equally lush. If you decide to forego a concert or other performance, wander around this beautiful place, have a coffee or drink at one of the cafes, and watch the panorama of activity. This is one place you can be part of the "madding crowd" or blissfully secluded at one of the outdoor or indoor cafes or just stroll through one of the less crowded plazas.

Day 2 🍙

Highlights: Walkways along the **East River, Beekman and Sutton Places**, a cable car ride, **Abigail Adams Smith Museum, Bloomingdale's** and a horse-drawn carriage ride.

Lunch at Le Train Bleu, Bloomingdale's, 1000 Third Ave. (6th floor) *Telephone 705-2100.*

Dinner at L'Ermitage. 40 W. 56th St. Reservations required: *Telephone 581-0777.*

Gardens, river enclaves, and a private cobblestone street are the locations for this early morning walk. Later, you will ride a cable car to see great views of the East River.

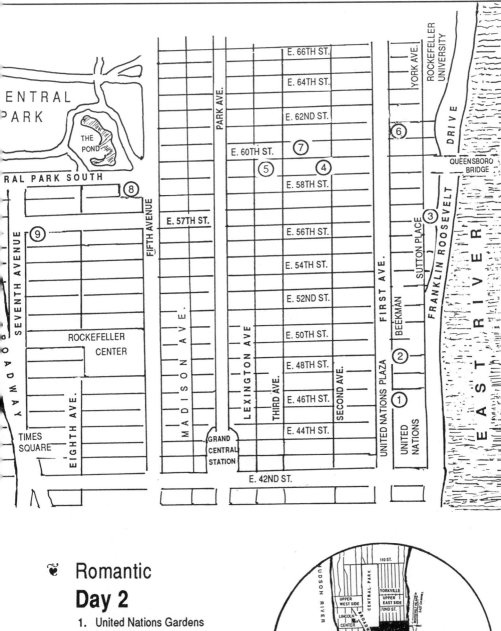

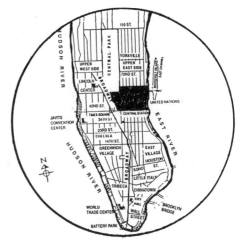

❧ Romantic
Day 2

1. United Nations Gardens
2. Beekman Place
3. Sutton Place
4. Cable Car station
5. Bloomingdale's
6. Abigail Adams Smith House
7. Serendipity Restaurant
8. Grand Army Plaza
9. Carnegie Hall

In the afternoon, your romantic strolls will lead you to an 18th-century home in the middle of the city. A horse-drawn carriage will take you through Central Park and drop you off a few blocks from an elegant Russian restaurant. This is romantic New York right in the middle of the bustling city!

Morning

① **B**egin your day in the **Public Gardens,** just north of the United Nations buildings at 46th St. next to the East River. A 48th St. entrance leads to a playground area, but adults can only be admitted here if they are in the company of a child.

This beautiful and secluded park is not usually busy with visitors. A **rose garden** runs between the river promenade and the east wall of the General Assembly building. On the lawn is **Vuchetich's** bronze statue, *Let Us Beat Our Swords Into Plowshares,* a gift of the U.S.S.R. A bronze equestrian, *Monument to Peace,* was presented by Yugoslavia.

Walk along the promenade. To the north is a memorial to Eleanor Roosevelt, a gift of the German Democratic Republic. You may have to look hard for this one; it is sort of hidden. Enjoy the river views as you walk.

Leave at the 46th St. exit, turn right about two blocks to Mitchell Place. **Beekman Tower** is on the corner. Turn right and ② walk up Mitchell to the quiet enclave called **Beekman Place,** located on a high bluff overlooking the river. At 51st St., turn right a few steps. The pedestrian foot bridge crosses FDR Drive. You can look down on the park and drive below you. There is a steep flight of steps which you can walk down to **Peter Detmold Park** and walk along the river if you choose. Be careful. The steps are steep, narrow and slippery when wet.

FDR Drive, rumbling along below you, was begun in 1936 and finished after World War II. The roadbed is filled with rubble from the London Blitz, brought back as ballast in returning American ships.

Walk back to First Ave., turn right, past the tile shop and fish place; past **L. Simchick's Meats and Poultry.** Note **Billy's 1870 bar and restaurant**, featuring gas light fixtures, wooden bar and walk-in freezer.

On 53rd turn right and follow the curve to **Sutton Place**, one of ③ the most elegant sections of the city. The blocks from here to 58th St. are filled with luxury apartments and townhouses, some sharing a common back garden. There are river overlooks at both 55th and 56th Sts. with the Queensboro Bridge on the horizon.

At the end of 57th St. is a small park with a replica of the boar, Il Porcellino, found in the Straw Market in Florence, Italy. Another small park is on the east end of 58th St. Just north of the 58th St. park and parallel to the river is a small private bricked street, **Riverview Terrace**, with five 19th-century houses covered with ivy. Note the column at the entrance with the figure of a goat.

Walk to 58th St., turn left past a pretty, private plaza to Second Ave. Turn right on Second Ave. to 59th for a wonderful and un- usual sightseeing trip, the **cable car** ride to **Roosevelt Island.** I ④ just suggest taking the ride over and back to get a good view of the **East River** and the **Queensboro Bridge.**

If you want to stay on the island and explore, look for the free red bus which meets the tram and takes you north up Main Street. The island was a farm in the 18th-century, owned by the Blackwell family; later it served as the site for a prison, an asylum, a poorhouse and hospitals.

Noon

Time for lunch at **Bloomingdale's**, located one block west on ⑤ 59th, between Third and Lexington Aves. After leaving the cable car station, walk one block east on 59th St. to Third Ave. Bloomie's is on the corner. Plan to explore the store after lunch.

Take the elevator up to the sixth floor for lunch at **Le Train**

Bleu. Here is your chance to eat on the Orient Express. Bloomie's has created a luxury French railway car, complete with green velvet chairs and carpeting and windows overlooking the Queensboro Bridge and the East River. The views are great, the ambience is terrific and the prices are moderate.

Afternoon

After lunch spend some time wandering around Bloomies. Most people think this is the most exciting department store in town, and maybe it is. You can visit the tasting bar/cafe in the basement, the room displays on the fifth floor, the dozens of little boutiques featuring designer clothes on the third floor, and the lingerie department with its pretty and expensive items.

Walk north on Third Ave. to 61st St., turn right. On your left is a square block known as the **Treadwell Farm Historic District**. This block will give you an idea of what this area looked like at the turn of the century. Note the brownstones and terraced houses.

(6) Continue another block and a half east on 61st to the **Abigail Adams Smith House** (1799) between First Ave. and York. Open Monday through Friday, 10 a.m. to 4 p.m., Sundays, 1 to 5 p.m. Admission. This 18th-century stone stable is one of only a handful of 18th century buildings in New York. Ring the bell to let the guide know you are there; if the weather is nice, she will suggest you wait in the pretty formal garden behind the house. Follow the brick walkway and enjoy the little formal garden, wooden benches and ivy, trained in formal designs, on the back wall. Tours are scheduled every hour and a half. This is a most unusual period piece to find in the middle of Manhattan.

Ice Cream Time. Walk west on 61st to Second Ave., turn left one block to 60th St., then right to 225 E. 60th and the popular (7) **Serendipity** for your afternoon refreshment stop. Diets are off. Two straws for the mammoth frozen hot chocolate or share any of their enormous sundaes or other good treats.

Late Afternoon

Walk one block south to 59th St., then west about four blocks to Fifth Ave. Here you are at the south east corner of **Central Park**, site of the **Grand Plaza** and the famous **Plaza** ⑧ **Hotel**.

Time for a ride in one of New York's horse-drawn **hansom cabs,** located along the south end of Central Park. The official rate is now $34 for the first half hour. Nothing you do in this city will beat a ride in one of these traditional horse drawn carriages.

Evening

Take a ride through the park on the most romantic trip in town. After your carriage ride, stretch your legs by walking south on Fifth Ave. to 56th St. turn right for one and a half blocks to L'Ermitage, 400 56th St., for first-rate food in a lovely setting. Ask for a table in the Garden Room on the second floor.

Enjoy a concert at Carnegie Hall and your second romantic day in Manhattan is coming to an end. Just in case you want a night-cap, take a cab across town to the **Carlyle Hotel** (35 E. ⑨ 76th St. at Madison Ave.). Bobby Short often plays piano in the **Cafe Carlyle** and jazz pianists play in the more relaxed and less expensive **Bemelmans Bar**. Note the murals painted by Ludwig Bemelmans when he was a waiter here. And so to bed.

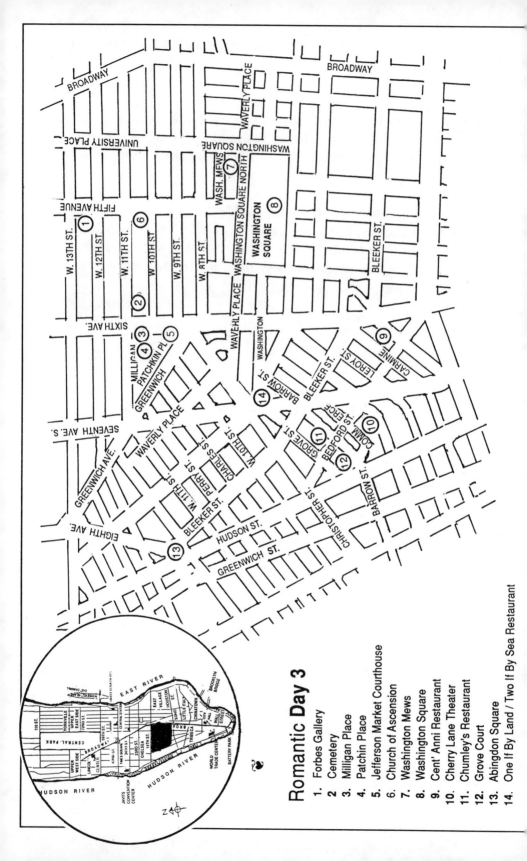

Romantic Day 3

1. Forbes Gallery
2. Cemetery
3. Milligan Place
4. Patchin Place
5. Jefferson Market Courthouse
6. Church of Ascension
7. Washington Mews
8. Washington Square
9. Cent' Anni Restaurant
10. Cherry Lane Theater
11. Chumley's Restaurant
12. Grove Court
13. Abingdon Square
14. One If By Land / Two If By Sea Restaurant

❦ Day 3

You will spend most of today in **Greenwich Village**. This was the United State's Left Bank during the 1920s, home to artists, writers, radicals and experimental theaters. Here were the Provincetown Players with Eugene O'Neill and Edna St. Vincent Millay. There lived e.e. cummings and John Reed and Theodore Dreiser. "My Sister Eileen" was in the center of town, Mayor Jimmy Walker lived on St. Luke's Place, and Dylan Thomas drank himself to death at the White Horse Tavern. Jazz clubs and cabarets introduced most of the 20th-century jazz artists. At some point during the first half of the century, Greenwich Village seemed like the center of the artistic and political world. All my life the name conjured up visions of freedom and art and made the places I lived seem prosaic and tame.

In addition to its political and artistic history, the village is filled with charming and romantic-looking buildings, cobbled streets, old gas lamps and an eclectic group of residents. And the restaurants aren't bad, either. It is a perfect place for a pair of romantics to spend a day. Incidentally, you do not walk through the village; you weave your way through. No grid of streets exist here. These winding cow paths of streets are exactly that — they followed the Indian paths, canals and trails of earlier days. It is easy to get turned around, but never lost. You will just explore new territory.

Highlight: Greenwich Village.

Reservations: Lunch: Cent'Anni, 50 Carmine St., between Bleecker and Bedford Sts. *Telephone 989-9494.* **Dinner: One If By Land, Two If By Sea**, 17 Barrow St. *Telephone 228-0822.*

Morning

At about 10 a.m., cab or bus to the corner of Fifth Ave. and 12th St., the northernmost point of **Greenwich Village.** Here you will find one of the most charming and least known galleries in New York, the **Forbes Gallery.** And it is free. 900 ① tickets are issued per day, first-come, first-served basis. Open

Tuesday through Saturday, 10 a.m. to 4 p.m.; closed Sunday and Monday. This was Malcolm Forbes' gift to New York and to you. It contains his collections of model boats, toy soldiers, historical documents and trophies and his fabulous treasures of Faberge eggs, boxes and other objets de luxe.

I suggest you start your third day in Romantic New York here, primarily to see the **Faberge eggs** in cases 18 through 28. You will see the incomparable gifts presented by the Russian czars to their wives and children. The first time I came to see the Faberge treasures, but I stayed, and now I return, to see the dioramas of toy soldiers and the exhibitions of model boats. The installations are superb, and believe it or not, they are musically scored.

Walk south on Fifth Ave. one block to Eleventh St. Turn right. Tenth and Eleventh Sts. are filled with handsome houses, lovely doorways, and impressive architectural details. Note **Number 18** with its modern projected window. This is the house that was destroyed by a bomb, accidentally detonated by members of the Weathermen, one of the more radical groups born during the 1960s. Its new design caused a great deal of concern on the part of preservationists. Note the doll in the window. According to my friends in the neighborhood, the doll changes clothes periodically to keep up with the times.

② Just before you arrive at Sixth Ave., you will pass a tiny triangular cemetery. This is the **second cemetery of the Spanish and Portuguese Synagogue** (1805). Most of it was destroyed when Eleventh St. was constructed, but this tiny remnant remains. The gate has always been padlocked when I have walked by, but you can peek in to see the very old stones.

③ At Sixth Ave. (Avenue of the Americas), cross the street, turn right a few steps and peek into **Milligan Place** where Eugene O'Neill lived. Basque waiters from the old Hotel Brevoort once lived here and, according to legend, so did the French feather workers who curled ostrich and egret plumes for ladies of fashion.

Around the corner on 10th St. is little **Patchin Place**, just op- ④
posite the old Jefferson Courthouse. Here lived Theodore
Dreiser, as well as John Reed, who wrote *10 Days That Shook The
World* and was the protagonist in Warren Beatty's movie, *Reds*.
e.e. cummings lived at Number 4 for 40 years, until his death in
1962. Remember the writer whose poetry sported no capital letters?

Across the street is perhaps the most fantastic and extraordinary building in New York, the **Jefferson Market Courthouse**, ⑤
now a branch of the New York Public Library. It has been at
times a market, a courthouse and a jail. Its history may be spot-
ty, but the building is magnificent, with turrets, towers, carvings, stained glass and gables. It is Victorian Gothic
architecture at its zenith. You can see a strange juxtaposition if
you look south on Sixth: there are the twin towers of the World
Trade Center as background for this exotic building.

Walk behind the library to see the **Jefferson Market garden**,
maintained by volunteers on weekends. You will see the signs
inviting you to join them. Even if the gates are locked, you can
see the paths, ivy, trees and roses as you walk around the building.

Walk east on 10th St., back toward Fifth Ave. The brownstones
from Numbers 20-38 are called the **English Terrace**. As you ⑥
walk along, notice the flower boxes, trees, grillwork and Number 14, where Mark Twain lived for a brief time.

Walk back to Fifth Ave. and the **Church of Ascension** (1840-41).
Take a minute to walk in to see the marble altar, the mural and
the remarkable stained glass windows, made of opalescent
glass. The church is open daily noon to 2 p.m. and 5 to 7 p.m.

Cross Fifth Ave. and walk a few steps west on Eleventh St. to
Number 7 to see an unusual East Indian teakwood bay window
(1887), probably the only town house in New York so
decorated.

Return to Fifth Ave., turn left and walk toward Washington

Square; you will see the famous **Arch** beckoning you on. Just
⑦ beyond Eighth St., you will see the **Washington Mews** on your
left. The buildings on the north side were stables. Today it is a
charming private alley. Walk up and down; at the far end notice
the German and French houses.

Just beyond the Mews on Fifth Ave. is a private building with a
wonderful garden. You cannot walk into the garden, but you
can enjoy it through the wrought iron fence. A sign reads,
"**Willy's Garden**. Living Memorial to William Carrieri (1906-
76). His skillful hands created this place of beauty. His warm
heart enriched those who knew him." This oasis is filled with
lavender, white and scarlet flowers.

⑧ Continue to and through **Washington Arch** and **Washington
Square Park**. The park is currently experiencing a renaissance
and the drug pushers are having to find a new home. Children
cavort in the playgrounds, people sun and converse, chess
players, roller skaters and students from nearby New York
University enjoy the park. Before you walk under the arch,
notice the figures of **Washington in War** and **Washington in
Peace** on either side. At the far side of the arch you can still see
a locked door which used to open to the stairway leading to the
top of the arch. No more. The arch has been recently cleaned
and is very handsome.Wander through the park, turn right and
exit on Washington Place West. **Number 82** was home to Willa
Cather.

Lunch

It is getting on time for lunch. Turn left on Sixth Ave., cross the
street and walk about two blocks south to Carmine St. You
are now in the Village's Italian neighborhood. Turn right and
walk about a block to Number 50 Carmine and the Italian res-
⑨ taurant, **Cent'Anni** (100 years). They serve excellent pasta from
tortelloni and fettucini to rigatoni and capellini, the lovely
angel hair pasta. Entrees may include several veal dishes, red
snapper and broiled game hen. Check the daily specials and
save room for dessert, such as tartufo ice cream, chocolate
mousse cake or a lovely apricot sorbet. Prices are moderate.

Afternoon

Walk west on Carmine St. to Seventh Ave., cross the street, turn right and walk one block to **St. Lukes Place**. This is a funny little curving section of a street next to Le Roy St. St. Lukes usually does not appear on any map.

Turn left on St. Lukes and walk down this street of pretty red bricked front houses built in the Italianate style of the 1850s. Mayor James J. Walker lived at **Number 6** from 1926 to 1933. The two lamps of honor in front of the house were the traditional Dutch way to mark the home of a mayor.

Walk back to Seventh Ave., turn left and go one block to Bedford St. Bedford angles off Seventh at a 45-degree angle; it is a bit confusing here. **Number 70 Bedford** was built in 1807. **Number 75 1/2** is the narrowest house in the Village, only nine and one-half feet wide. Edna St. Vincent Millay lived here for a year in 1923. A good deal of this property on Bedford St. was owned by Aaron Burr, Alexander Hamilton's nemesis. **Number 77**, at the corner of Bedford and Commerce Sts., is believed to be the oldest house in the Village (1799-1801). It has survived a number of alterations.

Turn left on Commerce St., around the curve, past the **Cherry Lane Theater**, founded by Millay and her friends; one of the first Off Broadway theaters called by that name. Walk past the **Grange Restaurant** on your left and the twin houses at **Numbers 41 and 39** on your right. According to legend, they were built by a sea captain for his two daughters who did not get along together, but a more pedestrian history says they were built for a milkman. I like the sea captain story better.

Turn right on Barrow St. one block to Bedford again. You really just went around the block. Time for a stop at the infamous **Chumley's**, New York's best-hidden and best-known speakeasy. You can enter from either Barrow or Bedford, if you know what to look for. Walk straight ahead on Barrow, look for the first opening to a courtyard on your left. Walk through a little stone-paved court to **Number 70** with its rounded grilled door and step down the small flight of steps into Chumley's. Or you can turn left onto Bedford and walk to Number 86 which is just a wooden grilled door with no name.

In either event, you will find yourself in this old smoky bar-room where F. Scott Fitzgerald, John Dos Passos and Theodore Dreiser hung out. If you happen by on a Saturday afternoon, you might stumble into a poetry reading.

⑫ Walk right on Bedford when you leave Chumley's, for half a block to Grove St. Turn left to Numbers 10 and 12, **Grove Court,** tucked away behind a gate and a passageway. Once known as Mixed Ale Alley, it is now a private living space, but you can see the lanterns and entrances through the locked gate. I have to admit that on occasion when the gate is open, I have quietly walked into the square. It is lovely and peaceful.

Back to Bedford and Grove Sts. where you will see one of the few remaining frame houses in the village (1822). Try to ignore the disfiguring fire escape. The little 1 1/2 story grey house with blue shutters behind **Number 17** was a workshop. Behind the frame house is **Twin Peaks** at Number 102 Bedford. It is one of the strangest houses in this village of strange buildings, a real Hansel and Gretel creation. The owner, Clifford Reed Daily, claimed to be disenchanted with buildings in the village and remodeled the house, in his words, as an "island growing in a desert of mediocrity."

Walk one block north on Bedford (or as north as Bedford runs at this point); you are now at Christopher St. with the famous **De Lys Theatre** across the street. Turn right past the Li Lac Candy Store at Number 120 with its exotic chocolate concoctions and McNulty's coffee and tea shop, established in 1895, across the street. Walk two blocks to W. Fourth St., turn left. Stop at **Tartine**, 253 W. 11th St. for French bistro food. Then just wander up W. 4th St. and enjoy its shops and pretty ambience. Continue about five blocks to 12th St. Take a good look at the corner of Fourth and Eleventh Sts. as you cross. This is the most like Paris of any place in the neighborhood

The **W. 4th St. block** between 11th and 12th Sts. with its great brownstone buildings has become a favorite with movie-makers. Walk up one side and down the other, back to Bank St. Turn right on Bank St. to Bleeker St. Before you turn, look straight ahead to see **Abingdon Square** and its brick pavements and playground. Walk south on **Bleeker St.**, enjoying the antique shops and pleasant surroundings. ⑬

Evening

Continue on Bleeker St. to Barrow St. and turn left to the romantic and charming restaurant, **One If By Land, Two If By Sea**, at 17 Barrow St., between Bleeker/Seventh Ave. (they converge at this point) and W. Fourth St. You will have to look carefully; the restaurant is not marked very well. It is open seven days a week, 4 p.m. to 4 a.m., for cocktails and piano music. Dinner is served from 5:30 p.m. until midnight, Sunday through Thursday and from 5:30 p.m. until 1 a.m., Friday and Saturday. It accepts all major credit cards. This beautifully restored 18th-century landmark carriage house was formerly owned by Aaron Burr. The restaurant is built on two levels; try to get a table on the balcony, but plan to have drinks on the first floor. Take time to explore the details of this lovely place: brick walls, brass chandeliers, primitive American paintings and beautiful bouquets of silk flowers. The continental cuisine is expensive, but this is such a special place that I recommend you indulge yourselves on this last night of your romantic tour of the city. ⑭

New York, New York. Could you find a more romantic town?

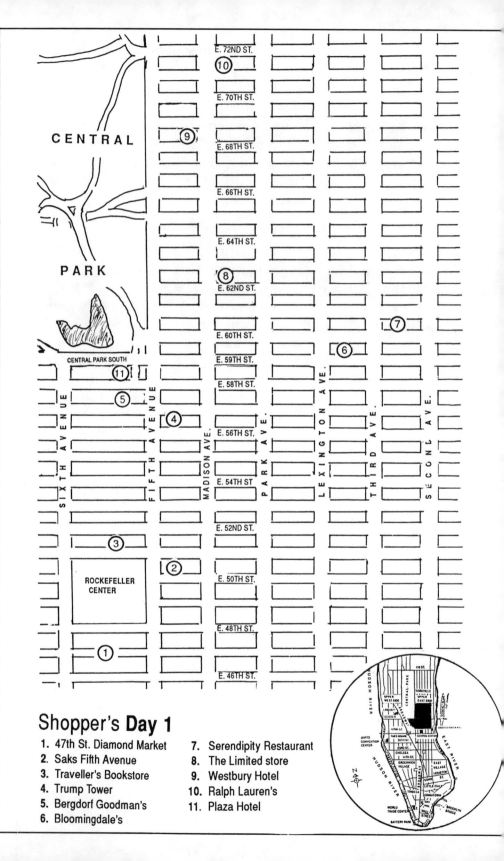

Shopper's **Day 1**

1. 47th St. Diamond Market
2. Saks Fifth Avenue
3. Traveller's Bookstore
4. Trump Tower
5. Bergdorf Goodman's
6. Bloomingdale's
7. Serendipity Restaurant
8. The Limited store
9. Westbury Hotel
10. Ralph Lauren's
11. Plaza Hotel

Shopper's New York

If you can't find it in New York City, they probably don't make it. This is a shopper's paradise, whether you are looking for bargains or prepared to spend a king's ransom. There are places you can bargain and others where you need to make an appointment before they will even open their doors to you.

This chapter is not aimed at finding the best buys in town; it is an attempt to introduce shoppers to the wide assortment of shopping available in this city, from the most elegant boutiques on Madison Ave. to the bustling markets on Orchard St.

Stores are usually open Monday through Saturday from 10 a.m. to 6 p.m. With the exception of the Lower East Side, most shops are closed on Sunday. Sunday is the big shopping day on the Jewish Lower East Side; on Sundays they even close Orchard St. to traffic. Many uptown shops are open for late-night shopping on Monday and Thursday.

One important add-on expense to remember is the 8 1/4 percent city sales tax.

During the past few years there has been a huge increase in street vendors, particularly on some of the more stylish shopping streets such as Fifth Ave. They are most unpopular with their neighbors since they clutter up the sidewalks with cut-rate products, such as $2 umbrellas, scarves and belts. Prices and overhead are low, but there are no returns or guarantees. Buy at your own risk.

Every sort of shopping imaginable is available, from Ralph Lauren's store in the magnificent Rhinelander mansion on Madison Ave. to racks of goods on Canal St. and from punk fashions in the East Village to Oriental goods in Chinatown. The museum gift shops have extraordinary merchandise and the auction houses offer unique opportunities to bid and buy. The food shops offer some of New York's greatest pleasures.

Finally, you can window shop to your heart's content. From Thanksgiving to New Year's, the animated store window displays on Fifth Ave. and the holiday street decorations are fabulous. Whatever your desire, it can be satisfied here. When the going gets tough, the tough go shopping.

Day 1

Highlights: The **Diamond Center, Fifth Ave. Bloomingdale's** and **Madison Ave.**

Reservations: Lunch at **Serendipity** 3. 225 E. 60th St. *Telephone 838-3531.* Or **Gino's.** 780 Lexington Ave. *Telephone 758-4466.* **Tea** at the **Palm Court, Plaza Hotel.** *Telephone 546-5350.* **Dinner** at **La Ripaille,** 605 Hudson St. *Telephone 255-4406.*

Morning

Start the day at the corner of **Sixth Ave. and 47th St.** Sixth Ave. is also known as the Avenue of the Americas, so-named by Mayor Fiorello LaGuardia in 1945 as a bow to the unity of the American Republics. If you look carefully you may be able to find some of the 800 metal disks representing the nations of the Americas, which were installed in 1960. New Yorkers continue to call it Sixth Avenue.

Forty Seventh St., from Sixth to Fifth Aves., is the city's
Diamond Center. Most diamond dealers in New York are ①
Jewish, many of them Hasidic Jews, originating from an 18th-
century mystical sect of Judaism in Poland. Jews gravitated to
the diamond business because they were excluded from many
other occupations, because their constant persecutions taught
them the eminently sensible precaution of having their wealth
in small portable forms such as diamonds, and because the
hours of the diamond trade are flexible enough to permit them
to follow their religious obligations.

Whether you are interested in buying diamonds or not, I think
you will find this a fascinating block. The black-frocked
Hasidim, with their long beards, dark suits and broad-
brimmed hats, bustle up and down the street; the small store
windows are filled with glittering diamond rings and neck-
laces; and you suspect all kinds of deals are being made. You
are probably right. If you are interested in buying diamonds, be
sure you know what you are doing and that you have done
some comparison shopping. The serious diamond trading
centers are not open to the public, but the stores are delighted
to help you with your shopping.

If you want to feel a bit on the inside, walk to 4 West 47th St.,
the **Jeweler's National Exchange.** It is filled with a large number of dealer's booths. Walk to the back of the room. On the left
you will find a flight of steps, which will lead you to the second
floor and a very small kosher restaurant, the Diamond Dairy,
with tiny tables and counters where you can eat your bagel and
watch what is going on downstairs through the glassed-in windows overlooking the floor.

One other place to stop along here is the **Gotham Book Mart** at
41 West 47th. This old, new and used book store, has been here
for more than 60 years. It is particularly rich in books on
theater, poetry and other arts.

When you arrive at **Fifth Ave.**, turn left and proceed north on
this famous street. You will cross back and forth several times
during your morning stroll. Barnes and Noble bookstore and

Mikomoto Pearls are on the west side at 48th St.

At 49th St. you will come to **Rockefeller Plaza** on your left and
② **Saks Fifth Avenue** across the street. Saks Fifth Avenue says it
all. It immediately conjures up images of designers, Vuitton
luggage, luxury foods and furs; all such images are correct.
This is a lovely store with helpful salespeople.

Take a few minutes to walk down the promenade, along the
Channel gardens to the plaza where, depending on the
weather, people will either be ice skating or eating in the summer restaurants. As you return to Fifth Ave., you will pass the
renowned Swiss chocolate shop, **Teucher's**. The decorations,
which change from season to season, may be the most extraordinary in town. Stick your head in and buy at least one of their
expensive champagne truffles.

Turn left on Fifth Ave., past the International Building with
Atlas holding up his world and **St. Patrick's Cathedral** across
the way.

At 51st St. you will find Versace's beautiful clothes and
Cartier's fabulous jewelry. 52nd St. brings the big book dealer,
B. Dalton.

Turn left on 52nd St. to Number 22, the Warner Communications Building. In the lobby you will find the excellent
③ **Traveller's Bookstore.** Here you will find not only travel books
for every country and city you can think of, but each section includes books on the art, geography, history, and gardens of the
country. They also include some appropriate fiction and non-
fiction books, as well as maps, dictionaries and walking guides.
For travel aficionados, this is a must.

Back to Fifth Ave. and St. Thomas' French Gothic Episcopal
Church at the corner of 53rd. Next come Fortunoff's jewelry
and silver store with surprisingly moderate, often discounted
prices; and **Gucci**, where nothing is moderate or discounted.
Even without moderation or discount, Gucci has been so successful it has opened a second store across the street.

Beyond 52 and 53 Sts. you can visit **Takashimaya,** the beautiful Japanese store; **Dior's;** the **Disney Store** and **Godiva,** where you can at least fill your eyes with the beautifully packaged and expensive chocolates.

At 55th St., **Steuben Glass** is more like a museum than a store. Wander through the dark rooms with the lighted display cases featuring their lovely engraved crystal.

Cross 56th St. to the amazing **Trump Tower.** Let the doorman ④ welcome you, then walk down the apricot-colored marble corridor to the wall of water. Escalate to the second floor to enjoy the views. Most of the stores are very expensive.

If you want a cup of coffee, this is the place to stop. It will cost more than most places, about $5 for a cup of coffee and a roll, but it is worth it to sit in the center of this temple devoted to conspicuous consumption and enjoy its lavishness. There are lots of little tables in front of the waterfall.

If you haven't had enough, next door is **Tiffany's.** I love Tiffany's, maybe because they are always so nice. One of my favorite New York memories is of watching a woman lead a dog on a leash through the crystal department at Tiffany's one day. I murmured to a salesperson that I wondered how rich you would have to be to walk a dog through all that expensive crystal. She said that if I thought the dog's collar was rhinestone, I was mistaken. Every once in a while I forget what real money is.

Bergdorf Goodman's store for men is on the east side; across ⑤ from the B and G store for women. This may be the ultimate in shopping and yet the most pleasant. The store has recently been remodeled and its boutiques are even more elegant. Its windows may be the best in town; and I love its shoe department where you can not only rest your feet, but find wonderful buys during sales. Across the street is the new Warner Brothers complex.

You are now at the **open space** on 58th St. with the Pulitzer

Fountain in front of you, the Plaza Hotel to your left and the ugly General Motors Building on your right. **F.A.O. Schwartz**, the great toy store, has moved to the General Motors Building. Its oversize elephants, bears and Raggedy Ann dolls have softened the building considerably.

Retrace your steps one block on Fifth Ave. to 57th St., and turn left at the **Warner Brothers Store**. This block has become a very strange mix of the ordinary and the extraordinary.

Just beyond the **Warner Brother's** store is the **Original Levi's Store**. No explanation necessary. Then past the designer **Escada**, the British **Burberry's** with its fabulous rainware, the chic Parisian **Hermes** and the newest addition to the block: the 16-story **Chanel**. This lavish building is reminiscent of Coco Chanel's legendary salon in Paris. It features satiny black display cases, Coromandel lacquer screens and a double staircase. A 12-foot Paris-made sofa made for the store had to be delivered via a third-story window.

Walk a block further to **Holland & Holland** at 50 East 57th St. Established in London in 1835, this is its first American presence. It is aimed at the gentleperson hunter and traveler with accessories for safaris and fancy rifles. It is somewhat amusing to see this very high-class store on the same block as **Victoria's Secret** and **Speedo**. Only in New York.

Continue east past Park Avenue and turn left on Lexington. ⑥ Continue down to 59th St. and **Bloomingdale's**.

Before you attack this shopping bastion, take time for lunch.

Noon

Two choices for lunch today. One is an old-fashioned ice cream parlor, which has been in the neighborhood for 30 years, and the other is an Italian restaurant, operated by the same owners for 42 years. Take your pick.

Gino's is at 780 Lexington Ave., across the street and a few steps from Bloomies. It begins serving at noon. This is a small Italian restaurant, vibrant with red wallpaper covered with cavorting zebras. Why, I have no idea. The host is a charmer; the food is good and the prices moderate. It is obviously a neighborhood place because everyone seems to know each other and many have their own tables. But they still make a stranger feel welcome. I discovered the owners are from the Naples/Capri area of Italy and since Capri is my favorite place in the whole world, at least the world I know, I was immediately prejudiced in their favor. The pasta is excellent.

Serendipity is the name of the ice cream parlor at 225 E. 60th ⑦ St., between Third and Second Avs. They define the name as the art of finding the pleasantly unexpected by chance or sagacity. You can claim sagacity. For some strange reason, this place has been a New York City landmark for years. Everybody comes. They sell trendy novelties in the front of the store. The restaurant with 32 tables is in the back of the first floor and on the second floor. You can try a reservation, but you will probably still have to wait. The Tiffany-like lampshades, round marble tables and white tiled floor are somehow enchanting. Their hamburgers are two inches high; exotic omelets feature white asparagus and chutney and the blue corn nachos are terrific. I love the Frrrozen Hot Chocolate...that's the way they spell it. It is frozen hot chocolate, served in a huge dish, heaped with whipped cream and dusted with chocolate. Get two straws and share. This place subscribes to the belief that more is more.

Afternoon

Back to **Bloomingdales**. What can I tell you? Everybody knows about Bloomies. It is filled with small shops, big shops, model rooms on the fifth floor, lingerie on the fourth, fabulous food shops and occasionally great sales. It seems that almost every week they are featuring some extravaganza or other throughout the store.

Don't try to organize this trip; just wander around from shop to shop and floor to floor. This is better without a plan. Incidentally, restrooms for ladies are on 4 and 7; for men on 5 and 7.

Walk two blocks west to Madison Avenue. The blocks between 59th and 61st Sts. have changed enormously in the past few years. Look to your right to see a large **Crate and Barrel** housewares store across the street.

On the west side of the street between 60th and 61st are **Barney's** and **Calvin Klein**. **Barney's** is an elegant store filled with what I call "black clothes" and **Klein's** is "installed" with the reverse: "white clothes."

At 61st you will find a second **Teucher's** chocolate shop, just east of Madison, where you can get the truffle you missed earlier in the day. Wipe your fingers and walk into **Royal Copenhagen** for Porcelain and **George Jensen** for silver if their new stores are completed. Visit **Julie's Artisan's Gallery** to see and try on her wearable art clothing.

⑧ The fabulous **Limited** is at 62nd St. No matter how many of these chain stores you have been in, take my word for it, this one is different. It looks a bit ordinary as you walk in, but walk to the back of the store. On your left are five circular flights of steps under a huge skylight, surrounded by mirrors. A video show will be underway on the ground floor. Walk the stairs and check out the trendy clothes on the upper floors. On your way out, look in the lingerie shop at the side of the main floor.

Floris, the great London perfumery, has opened a shop at 703 Madison. At 713 Madison is the **Waterford/Wedgewood** shop with its crystal and china, great chandeliers and charming salespeople. **Erica Wilson's** Needleworks is on the second floor at Number 717.

Between 66th and 67th is **Nicole Miller's** clothing. **Berk's**, an immigrant from the Burlington Arcade in London, is filled with lovely cashmeres and woolens. Between 67th and 68th Sts., you will find **Godiva Chocolates** and **Frette's** amazing bedding.

Between 68th and 71st Sts. you will find the fabulous **Valentino** store; **Missoni** clothing and **Cartier's** extraordinary jewelry located in the Westbury Hotel, **Jaeger's** new clothing store and the marvelous **MacKenzie Child** with glorious painted ceramics. **Mabel's** is filled with objects and furniture featuring all kinds of painted or carved animals.

We're not done yet. **Saint Laurent's** Parisian clothing and **Pierre Deux's** original fabrics are also located in this area.

I have saved the most incredible for last. Across the street is **Ralph Lauren's** newest store in the renovated Rhinelander mansion. Filled with dark wood, wonderful stairways, family portraits, carpeting, draperies and baskets of flowers, it is a shopper's delight. The epitome of luxury and subdued ostentation.

You could continue walking and shopping for 20 more blocks north on Madison, but this seems a good place to stop to regroup. If you want continued ostentation as you rest, walk back two blocks to the Westbury Hotel, between 69th and 70th Sts, to **The Polo** restaurant where the ladies lunch and relax in mid-afternoon. Or hail a cab to **The Plaza** for tea in the Palm Court. I opt for the Plaza. Your pastries, open sandwiches, strawberries, cakes and tea can be enjoyed at a moderate cost. The violin and piano music is guaranteed to soothe you.

Evening

This evening you will want to rest your tired feet. After tea, go back to your hotel to shower and relax. Tonight cab to a little restaurant in Greenwich Village named **La Ripaille**, French for "festive occasion" or "feast." Located at 605 Hudson, just off 12th St., it seats about 45 people around its small tables. Notice the grandfather clock, brick and stucco walls, old fireplace and small bar. The specials are different every day. I love their lamb, no matter how it is prepared, and the vegetable mousse. I always save room for dessert. They do such special things with white chocolate, it is almost indecent. A dinner in this pretty place with its excellent food at moderate prices should prepare you for the energetic, noisy and exciting shopping day to come tomorrow.

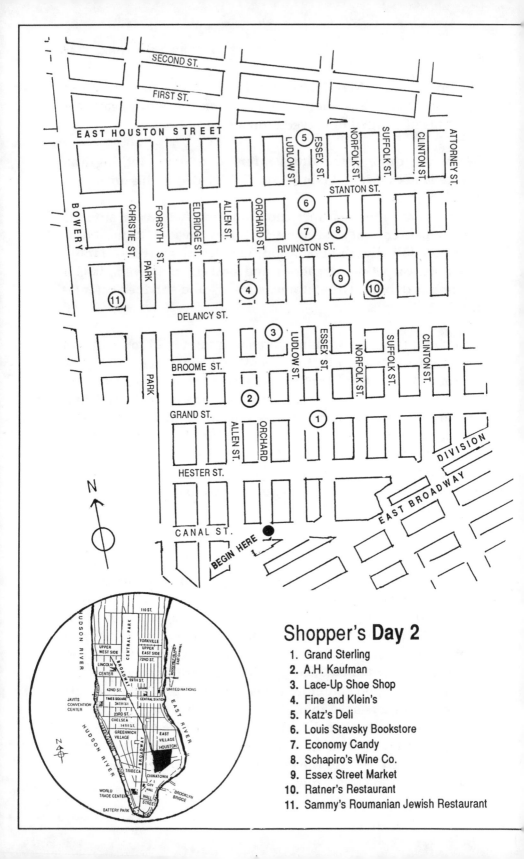

Shopper's **Day 2**

1. Grand Sterling
2. A.H. Kaufman
3. Lace-Up Shoe Shop
4. Fine and Klein's
5. Katz's Deli
6. Louis Stavsky Bookstore
7. Economy Candy
8. Schapiro's Wine Co.
9. Essex Street Market
10. Ratner's Restaurant
11. Sammy's Roumanian Jewish Restaurant

Day 2

Highlights: Shopping on the **Lower East Side**.

Reservations: Dinner: **Sammy's Roumanian**, 157 Chrystie St. *Telephone: 673-0330.*

Shopping in New York takes many forms. Yesterday you saw retail shopping at its most elegant and expensive. Today you will visit the **Lower East Side,** where the garment trade, sweatshops and pushcarts became a way of life for Jewish immigrants at the turn of the century, and where you can still get it wholesale. Much of the wholesale business moved to midtown before World War II, but the streets here are still teeming with stores, stalls and clothing racks.

From the 1880s to 1923, almost two million Jews immigrated from Russia, fleeing the pogroms and persecutions which followed the assassination of Tsar Alexander II in 1881. Untrained and uneducated, they turned to peddling or the "needle trades," one of the few options open to them. Eventually, their pushcarts moved over to Orchard Street, where they operated until 1938 when they were banned by the city. By then, many of the owners had purchased small shops along the street, which they extended by setting up stalls outside their front doors. It is these shops and stalls you will visit today. Since many shops are operated by Orthodox Jews, they close early on Friday and are closed on Saturday, for the Jewish Sabbath, but are open on Sunday, although many of them close on Sunday in the summer. On Sunday, Orchard St. becomes a pedestrian mall from Houston to Grand Sts., free of traffic.

This is a retail market with wholesale prices. You will find discounts from 20 to 50 percent off list price. If you want to bargain for still better prices when buying in quantity, do it quietly and be prepared to pay with cash.

Recommendation: If you really want to shop and buy, do not come on Sunday. The streets are jammed and there are often lines outside the more popular shops. If, on the other hand, you

want to have one of the most colorful and exciting shopping experiences in town, come on Sunday.

Caveat. I will name some of the shops in the area which I have
particularly liked for one reason or another. However, the
neighborhood is changing so rapidly that stores close almost
overnight. Be assured there are plenty of places to explore,
even if some of my favorites are no longer there. One of the exciting things about New York is its changing face.

Morning

Start your day by taking a cab to the corner of **Canal and Orchard** Sts. You can get here by bus or subway, but they are
both inconvenient and too complicated to try to figure out on a
short trip.

At the corner of Canal and Orchard Sts., notice the tall building, once a bank built by Sender Jermulowsky, one of the
Hester St. pushcart dealers. In the Panic of 1907, the bank col-
lapsed, taking with it the money and hopes of thousands of immigrants. As you walk along Orchard St., you will notice that
each block tends to be filled with stores and stalls handling
similar kinds of goods. For example, in the block between
Hester and Grand, you will find a number of stores handling
hosiery, socks and panty hose.

Turn right on Hester St. for two blocks to Ludlow St. There you
will find the wonderful **Sweet Life**, filled with candy, nuts,
dried fruits, coffees and lovely people. They have beautiful
foil-covered candies with images of flowers, fish, cats and even
soccer balls. You can find just the right gift for a friend at home
or for yourself.

Just beyond Sweet Life on Hester St. is the old-fashioned
Gertel's Bakery, with kugels, matzohs and pastries.

Back to Orchard St., where you will find the wonderful
Salwen's at 45 Orchard, between Hester and Grand Sts. This
"house of umbrellas, leather wallets, leather handbags, gloves

and gift items" has been in business through three generations. As you enter, you may hear "Irving" playing the violin. He often sits in the back of the store playing his beloved music while his wife, Beatrice, will regale you with tales of the Lower East Side and the businesses along Orchard St. If you can leave without at least one of their wonderful umbrellas, you have more self-control than I do.

At Grand St., turn left to **Fishkin's** at 314 and 318 Grand, featuring discounted designer clothes.

Back to Orchard, cross over and continue on Grand to 345 and **Grand Sterling** with its remarkable reproductions of antique ① silver religious objects as well as silver tableware. They stock some of the loveliest pieces I have seen in a shop. The owners are extremely helpful.

Back to Orchard, turn right. **A. W. Kaufman** with fine women's ② lingerie and excellent discounts is at 73 Orchard. Visit **Louis Chock**, in business since 1921 with his "hosiery, underfashions, sleepwear for the whole family." Be sure to pick up his catalog.

Across the street are **Forman's** bargain basements with clothes for "plus" sizes, and at Numbers 78-82 is their coat annex and designer apparel. Cross Broome St. for **Forman's petites** at 94.

The **Lower East Side Tenement Museum** has opened at 97 Orchard. It offers walking tours, exhibitions and programs year-round. Take a minute to climb its steep steps to explore the history of this part of New York.

The fanciest Orchard St. store is **Klein's of Monticello** at No. 105. Beautiful, expensive women's clothes and lots of "attitude." 110 is the home for the **Lace-up Shoe Shop**, with good ③ discounts.

Cross wide Delancey St. Number 119 may be the most famous of the Orchard St. shops, **Fine and Klein's**. Everybody I know, ④ who is a New York shopper, has a handbag from this shop. It has a wonderful leathery smell and is always crowded with shoppers looking for the perfect bag with a 20 percent discount. More bags and jewelry are on the second floor.

Altman's Luggage is at Number 135 and **Beckenstein's** at 125 has extraordinary fabrics for men's suits and shirts. They also have another store across the street featuring decorating fabrics. Continue on up the street, past **Rivington**, past **Stanton**, just wandering into any shop that looks interesting. You will start to notice stores handling fur coats.

Lunch

You are now at Houston St. (pronounced How-ston, Heaven knows why), the northern end of Orchard St. Time for a **late lunch**. By now, it should probably be about 1 p.m. Turn right one block to Houston and Ludlow and the famous **Katz's** delicatessen. Take a ticket from the woman near the door and walk over to the counter and order your lunch, cafeteria style. The huge men behind the counter will slice pastrami or corned beef to your order. The sandwiches are so big, you may want to share one. You can order big, salty French fries and cream soda; you will get big, juicy pickles. Take your tray to one of the tables located in the center of this huge place; the tables up against the walls are for waiter service. Remember this is the "When Sally Met Harry" movie place. "I'll have what she's having" was the great, memorable line.

Afternoon

Walk east to Essex St. and turn right. Between Stanton and Rivington you will come to 147 Essex and **Louis Stavsky Company**. Wander through to see their great selection of religious articles and books, including a large collection of Hebrew and Yiddish tapes. They also have some history and guide books about the Lower East side.

At 108 Rivington on your right is the **Economy Candy Store**. Test your resistance by wandering through this incredible maze of sweets. Left on Rivington 126 is **Schapiro's Wine Company**. If you happen to be here on a Sunday, you can take one of their free wine-tasting, half-hour long tours, from 10 a.m. to 6 p.m. In business since 1899, it is now the only winery in Manhattan. Whether it is Sunday or not, they are usually only too glad to give you a taste of their Kosher wine.

Back to Essex St. The block between Rivington and Delancey is filled with the enclosed **Essex Street Market**. This became the home for the pushcart merchants after they were banned from the streets in 1938. Today it is filled with all sorts of merchandise. This is my least favorite part of the shopping neighborhood. A quick look is probably all you will want.

Walk west on either side of Delancey. Visit any of the dozens of shops which line this broad street. When you arrive at Orchard St., depending on the time, you can do some more exploring. At the corner of Orchard and Delancey Sts., you are just four blocks from the restaurant where you will be eating supper.

Dinner

Sammy's Roumanian Jewish Restaurant is located at 157 Chrystie St. near Delancey St.; it's not kosher, but it's fun. Actually it is sort of like a big joke and no one has more fun with the joke than the folks who run it. You will be tempted to back out when you arrive and notice the depressing neighborhood, drooping decorations and shabby walls covered with photos and business cards. Be brave.

You have to make up your mind that this is going to be a New York experience and determine to have a good time. And it is hard not to be infected by the good-natured crowd that hangs out here. Ignore the house wine and mix up an egg cream from the seltzer, chocolate syrup and milk placed on each table. A sign, posted near the entrance, reads "No carbonic interplay allowed. Kindly confine all spritzing to the glasses. Offenders will have their seltzer revoked."

The food not only sticks to your ribs, but to your arteries; this is cholesterol heaven. Ignore your diet and everything you know about nutrition. For this one evening, just enjoy the east

European cooking that features stuffed everything, chicken fat and garlic. It is fun! There is usually violin and piano music; often a sing along develops, depending on the crowd. Relax and enjoy; this place cannot be duplicated.

Later, if you can move, you might want to try one of the jazz clubs in Greenwich Village. Have the restaurant folks get you a cab. **The Blue Note** is at 131 W. 3rd at Sixth Ave. and has sort of a traditional type of jazz. **Sweet Basil's** is at 88 7th Ave. between Bleecker and Grove Sts, with good contemporary jazz, and the famous **Village Vanguard,** at 178 7th Ave. at 11th St., runs the gamut from Dixieland to folk music and blues. A good way to end a unique and fascinating day in New York.

Day 3

Today you will visit the most eclectic shopping area in New York, **Soho.** Once the center of avant garde artist lofts and cooperative kitchens, this is now so "in" it is almost "out," but it is still more fun that most places.

Today you will find elegant restaurants, wearable art, old buildings, trucks and expensive art galleries. Stores of all kinds are tucked into unlikely places; this is about 30 square blocks of wonderment and surprise.

Plan to spend the whole day here, leisurely moving from one block to another. Since most places do not open until 11 a.m., plan to start a little later than usual this morning and shop a little longer.

Caveat: Galleries and shops move in and out of this area so rapidly that it is almost impossible to be totally accurate about just where everybody will be at any given moment.

Highlight: Soho.

Reservations: Dinner: L'Ecole, restaurant of The French Culinary Institute, 462 Broadway. Reservations: 219-3300.

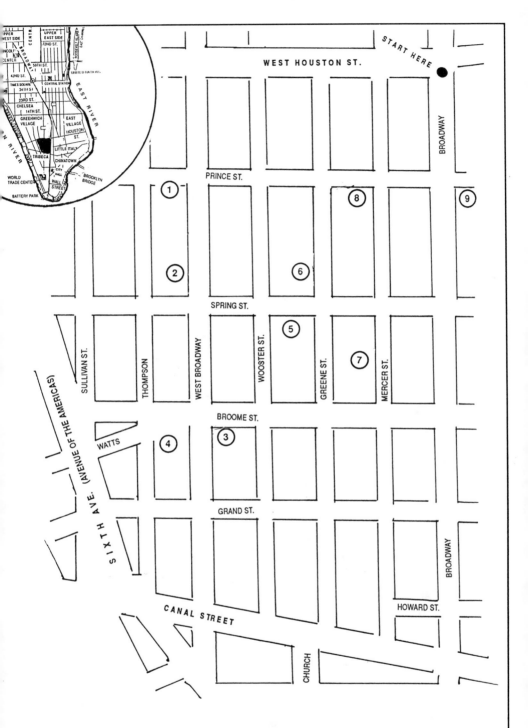

WEST HOUSTON ST.

START HERE

PRINCE ST.

SPRING ST.

BROOME ST.

GRAND ST.

CANAL STREET

HOWARD ST.

BROADWAY

SIXTH AVE. (AVENUE OF THE AMERICAS)

SULLIVAN ST.

THOMPSON

WEST BROADWAY

WOOSTER ST.

GREENE ST.

MERCER ST.

BROADWAY

CHURCH

WATTS

Shopper's
Day 3

1. Vesuvio's Bakery
2. Castelli's art gallery
3. The Cupping Room Cafe and Bar
4. Nacho Mama's Brewery
5. Japp Rietman (Second floor)
6.
7. Enchanted Forest shop
8. Fanelli's Bar
9. Dean & De Luca's store

Morning

Start your day at the corner of **West Houston and West Broadway.** Take a cab. The subway and bus routes are difficult to negotiate in this area.

Rizzoli's book store with an unusual doorway and great selections is at 454 N. Broadway. Be sure to visit its second floor. **Sally Hawkins Gallery,** with her oversized gems, is at the corner of West Broadway and Prince St.

(1) Turn right on Prince St. **Vesuvio Bakery** at 160 Prince is a Soho landmark. No sugar or preservatives; just the best Italian bread in the neighborhood. Across the street is **Cafe Borgia.** Stop for your morning capuccino when it opens about 10 a.m.

Retrace your steps to **West Broadway. Lulu's** at 436 W. Broadway is filled with wonderfully avant garde clothes. Across the street is **Dapy's** at 431 with neon and modern wares. 420 W.
(2) Broadway is home to several art galleries, including **Castelli, Charles Cowles** and **Sonnabend.** Many more galleries are in 415. **Ad Hoc Software** at 410 sells articles for the home and personal items, plus great paper goods.

Continue down West Broadway for an eclectic group of stores and restaurants. **Origins,** with its sweet-smelling skin care products, is at number 402; **Robert Lee Morris** and his spectacular jewelry is at number 400, and oddest of all in the middle of Manhattan is a **Smith & Hawken** garden store. They tell me they have the largest sales per square inch of store of any of the shops in their chain.

Anthropologie is at 375 W. Broadway with clothing, housewares, bath and kitchen "things." Very hip. And Across the street at number 376 is **Downtown,** Harry Cipriani's pretty and pricey new Venetian restaurant, right next to a garage. Soho can be strange.

Noon

Time to eat. To your right at Broome St. is the newly named Nacho Mama's Brewery offering burritos, fresh-lime margaritas and micro-brewed beers. Grilled steaks and chicken are also on the menu. Climb up the stairs to explore this former brewery. ④

At the corner of West Broadway and Broome, you will find **The Cupping Room Cafe and Bar**, 359 West Broadway, open seven days a week. This is one of my favorite restaurants in the neighborhood. It has been around for a while, is frequented by the locals and serves very good food at decent prices. They have the best sour cream muffins I have ever tasted; ask to have them toasted. You can get good salads, omelets, waffles, pasta and sandwiches. ③

Afternoon

Walk east on Broome St. At 484 is a dramatic furniture showroom, **Dialogica**, with green velvet walls and modern fabrics, rugs, chairs and tables.

Turn left on Wooster street. **Portico**, with its amazing home furnishings, is at 65 Wooster. It also has a second entrance at 379 W. Broadway, which you may have stumbled across. Across the street at 80 is **Gallery Henoch**, one of my favorites and at the corner of Wooster and Spring is a small outdoor market, which seems to operate even in the most dismal winter weather.

At the corner of Spring and Wooster is **Tennessee Mountain** rib restaurant, housed in a small wood-faced building, looking strangely out of place among all this cast iron. Turn right. At 131 Spring, you will find **Grass Roots Garden** on the first floor with green plants, huge pots and vases, and on the lower level, the **Grass Roots Gallery**, featuring Latin American and Haitian Folk Art.

Across the street at 134 is **Japp Rietman** for art books; climb to the second floor. Then go east to Green St.; turn left. At 93 ⑤

⑥ Green St., look in at **Shabby Chic Furnishings**, with trendy ideas and oddly fitting slip covers on furniture; on to **Zona's** at 97 to explore all her decorative items and Soleri bells and furniture.

⑦ Walk back to Spring St., turn left (east) and continue to Mercer. Turn right for half a block to **The Enchanted Forest** at 85 Mercer, a shop they describe as a "gallery of beasts, books and handmade toys celebrating the spirit of the animals, the old stories and the child within." This place is hard to resist with its overhanging trees, huge toy animals, little hiding places and wonderful books.

⑧ Walk north on Mercer, one and a half blocks to Prince St. where you will find **Fanelli's Bar**, the most Soho of all Soho bars. Stop for a glass of cold ale or a soft drink and enjoy the photos of the old boxing matches, a reminder that this used to be the haunt of fight fans.

Take a few minutes to walk north to 149 Mercer and the shop **After the Rain** to see its kaleidoscopes and fine crafts.

⑨ Back to Prince and one block east to Broadway where you will find the amazing **Dean and De Luca's** at 560. You could spend hours here roaming around the gorgeous food, cookware, books and talking to the most knowledgeable people about their wares. It is quite amazing. I counted eight kind of olives in brine, including Lebanese, Moroccan, and French provincial; about 40 kinds of bread, from regular semolina to rosemary and red pepper and the skinniest of sourdoughs. The vegetable mart is worth a few minutes with its exotic mushrooms, chestnuts, carmabola star fruits and organic Israeli tomatoes. If you can get out of there without a loaf of chunky peasant bread, an imported cheese or a pastry, you have stronger will power than I have.

I know this is the shopping chapter, but since you are here in the neighborhood and just a block away from my favorite building in New York, I am going to recommend a detour. Walk one block north on Broadway to Bleeker St., turn right for one short block. Across the street is the **Bayard-Condict Building,** the only Manhattan building designed by the great Chicago architect, Louis Henry Sullivan. Its intricately decorated terra cotta curtain wall is amazing, but it is the six angels at the top that make it really extraordinary to me. In order to see them, lean up against the dirty building on this side of the street and look upward to the top of the Bayard-Condict Building. You will see the angels with outstretched wings appearing to hold fragile hands as they loom over the street. I always stop to see them if I am in the neighborhood. Somehow, I feel better knowing that these angels are watching over the city.

Evening

There are dozens of restaurants in this area, but I chose one which is quite singular: **L'Ecole,** The French Culinary Institute at 462 Broadway near Grand St. This charming place is run by students, offers a five-course prix fixe menu after 8 p.m., which was recently priced at $22 and may be the best bargain in town. Consider: the students are trained by such chefs as Jacques Pepin, ex-chef to deGaulle, and Lutece's Andre Soltner.

Menus change every day, but to give you an idea of what you might expect, one dinner included the following: cream of fennel soup, Roquefort souffle, fillet of sole with cider, apples and cream, Pennsylvania Quail roasted and stuffed with rice, pommes Gaufrette, mango and apple tart with puff pastry or white and dark chocolate mousse. It is quite remarkable. Please make a reservation so you will not be disappointed.

If you have an early dinner, you will still have time to cab uptown to the theater for a play, concert or movie, but only after you have deposited your day's purchases in your hotel room.

These three tours in very different neighborhoods in New York should give you a taste for exploring the almost endless variety of shopping opportunities still awaiting you in this remarkable city.

Art
Day 1

A.M.

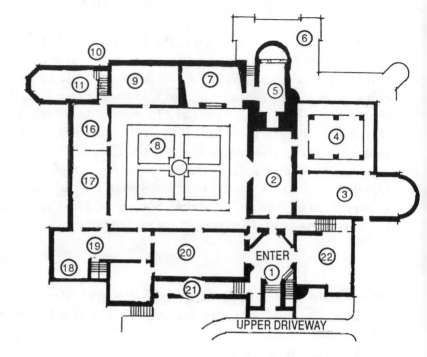

1. Entrance Hall
2. Romanesque Hall
3. Fuentaduena Chapel
4. St. Guilhem Cloister
5. Langon Chapel
6. West Terrace
7. Chapter House from Pontaut
8. Cuxa Cloister
9. Early Gothic Hall
10. Stairway to lower level
11. Gothic Chapel
12. Glass Gallery
13. Treasury
14. Trie Cloister
15. Bonnefont Cloister
16. Heroes Tapestry Room
17. Hall of the Unicorn Tapestries
18. Boppard Room
19. Tapestry Hall
20. Late Gothic Hall
21. Froville Arcade
22. Shop

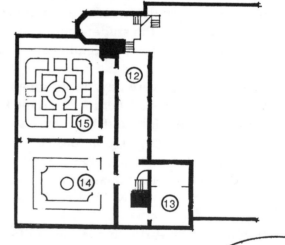

THE CLOISTERS

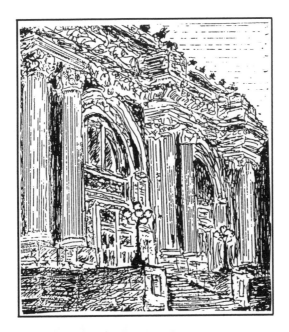

Art Lover's New York

In a city with more than 150 museums and 400 art galleries, a three-day tour is not much more than an appetizer. In addition there are hundreds of auction houses, libraries, corporate collections and works of art in public spaces. You could spend a lifetime exploring just the art collections in the city.

I subscribe to the belief that when looking at art, less is more. If you see 400 objects, you will remember none of them; if you see 20, you may remember 12. The following three days should be regarded as just an appetizer to a gargantuan feast still awaiting the visitor, but a very good appetizer.

During these three days you will visit the **Cloisters** with its medieval collection of objects and buildings, the monumental **Metropolitan Museum of Art**, the **Museum of Modern Art**, the **American Craft Museum** and some of the **galleries in Soho**. In each museum, you will visit a limited number of galleries and concentrate on a few of my favorite works of art or those which I suspect are the most important. One caveat: Museums are living, changing entities: objects may be moved, conservation laboratories may be restoring a work of art or an object may be on loan. Take heart, there are plenty left to enjoy.

You will pay an admission price or a suggested donation. Ticket prices are nominal, one of the best buys in town. Most of the museums you will visit also have inexpensive cafeterias or other kinds of restaurants. The food is usually very good.

Check open and closing times carefully. Traditionally, most museums throughout the world are closed on Monday. This is true in New York with one singular exception: **The Museum of Modern Art** is closed on Wednesday. Most galleries are closed on Monday; some are closed on Saturday and Sunday.

Day 1

Highlights: The Cloisters and **Cooper Hewitt Museum**.

Reservations: Lunch: **Sarabeth's**. 1295 Madison Ave. *410-7335*. Dinner: **Jezebel**, 630 Ninth Ave. at 45th St. *Telephone 582-1045*.

Morning

This is one of the few days on which I encourage you to take a subway ride. **The Cloisters** is at the northernmost end of the island, at 190th St. Leave early, so you will arrive about 9:30 a.m. when the museum opens. Buses are slow and a cab would be expensive. Get a few extra tokens for use on your bus rides later today.

Take the **A Train** (IND 8th Ave. Express) from any number of stops, 34th (Pennsylvania Station), 42nd (Times Square), Columbus Circle, or 72nd and Broadway, to 190th St. Remember Duke Ellington's famous rendition of Billy Strayhorn's "Take the A Train"? Well, this is what they were singing about. Get your subway token ($1.50 at this writing) and if you need help, ask the ticket seller for directions. The trip takes about 20 minutes from 59th to 190th St.

When you get off the train at **190th St.**, take an elevator to the street level. Turn right and you will be facing the entrance to **Tryon Park**, site of The Cloisters museum. The museum is open Tuesday through Sunday, 9:30 a.m. to 5:15 p.m. Closed Monday. You can either walk through the park to the museum or take the Number M4 bus up the hill. I recommend the bus.

Tryon Park's 66 acres are filled with terraces, lawns, gardens, Fort Tryon and gorgeous views of the Hudson River. If you decide to walk, and I warn you, it is a long walk, follow the footpath past the gardens, including the newly planted heather garden, the cafeteria, open from 10 a.m. to 5 p.m., and past the fort to the entrance to The Cloisters.

George Grey Barnard assembled most of this collection before World War I, including sections of cloisters from four medieval monasteries. Later John D. Rockefeller provided funds to permit the Metropolitan Museum of Art to purchase the collection, gave the Fort Tryon property to the city for the museum and contributed 42 objects from his collection to the project. He even went so far as to purchase land on the other side of the Hudson River and restrict development on it in order to preserve the view from the Cloister's terraces and gardens.

Many parts of the building are copies of medieval architecture, but have been designed and executed so beautifully, they are unobtrusive. Note the Belgian blocks on the courtyards; they were taken from old New York streets and reinstalled here.

The **entrance door** is at the lowest level of the building. Walk ①
up a flight of steps to the museum. Ask for a map when you purchase your tickets. Donations are requested.

Just beyond the entrance Hall is the **Romanesque Hall** with ②
magnificent doorways and frescoes.

To your right is the **Fuentiduena Chapel** from Spain with its ③
wonderful frescoes and the **St. Guilheim Cloister** with its ④
strange columns. Next you come to the comparatively modern Langon Chapel and its huge doors.

⑤ Just beyond the **Langon Chapel** walk down a small flight of steps to a wooden door which is often propped open; if not turn the round door handle to open. Don't push or pull; just turn. I always forget this.

⑥ Walk out on the **West Terrace**, overlooking the Hudson River. I think this is one of the most beautiful sights in this city of beautiful sights. I love to walk along the ramparts here to enjoy the view which has changed so little over the years.

⑦ Back into the museum. On your right is the **Chapter House** from Pontaut in the French Pyrenees with mostly original stones from the 12th-century. Notice the lovely carvings of birds, leaves and flower forms.

⑧ All the time you have been walking in and out of these chapels, you have been skirting the great **Cuxa Cloister** with its carved columns and pretty garden. The crossed paths with a fountain in the center is typical of a medieval enclosed yard. In the winter, the open arcades are glazed and the walkways are filled with potted plants.

⑨ The **Early Gothic Hall** is filled with 13th and 14th century statues including a seated ivory Madonna.

⑩⑪ At this point you will come to a stairway which leads you down to the **Gothic Chapel** and its Spanish tomb figures. Notice the animals resting at the feet of the figures: a pug dog for Don Alvaro de Cabrera and a lion for Jean d'Alluye.

⑫ Just beyond the chapel is the **Glass Gallery** with more than 75 panels and roundels of stained glass suspended in the windows. There is a wonderful sculpture of a female saint with rosy cheeks and a patterned cape, looking extremely disdainful as she reads from her book.

⑬ Then you come to **The Treasury**, which holds illuminated manuscripts, carvings and religious objects. Note the Books of Hours, particularly the Belles Heures of the Duc de Berry; and the Antioch Chalice from the 4th or 5th century.

Now it is time to visit the **two cloisters** on this lower level. First (14) is the Trie Cloister with the sound of its splashing fountain and the Stations of the Cross. All the plants here are to be found in the Unicorn Tapestries you will see upstairs.

Then the **Bonnefont Cloister**, filled with more than 250 plants (15) and herbs cultivated in the Middle Ages. The intricately arranged garden is divided by low wattle fences, protecting the plants and quince trees. There are resting benches where you can sit and enjoy the garden and the views of the Hudson River, and be startled by the sound of planes flying overhead.

Back up the stairs you walked down earlier, to the fabulous (16) tapestry rooms. **The Nine Heroes Tapestries** feature the figures and exploits of King Arthur, Julius Caesar, Hector, Alexander, David, Joshua, Judas, Charlemagne and the least known, to our generation, Godfrey of Maccabeus. Separated for centuries, most of this set of weavings has been brought together here in the Cloisters.

Lastly, in the next room are the most famous objects in the Cloisters' collections, the **Unicorn Tapestries**. Whether you (17) want to view them religiously, with the unicorn as symbolic of the Savior or as an allegory of courtly love, you cannot fail to be overwhelmed by the beauty of these weavings. Take some time to examine the details of flowers, animals, and human figures, as well as the pure and bright colors. These are truly masterpieces.

The Boppard Room is filled with stained glass and the **Burgos** (18)
Tapestry Hall with tapestries.
(19)

On your right, next to the Gothic Hall, is the **Froville Arcade**, (20) sporting nine arches.
(21)

You could exit from the Arcade to the Upper Drive. But if you (22) continue straight ahead you will be back in the entrance hall and the shop featuring books and reproductions. It is worth a visit.

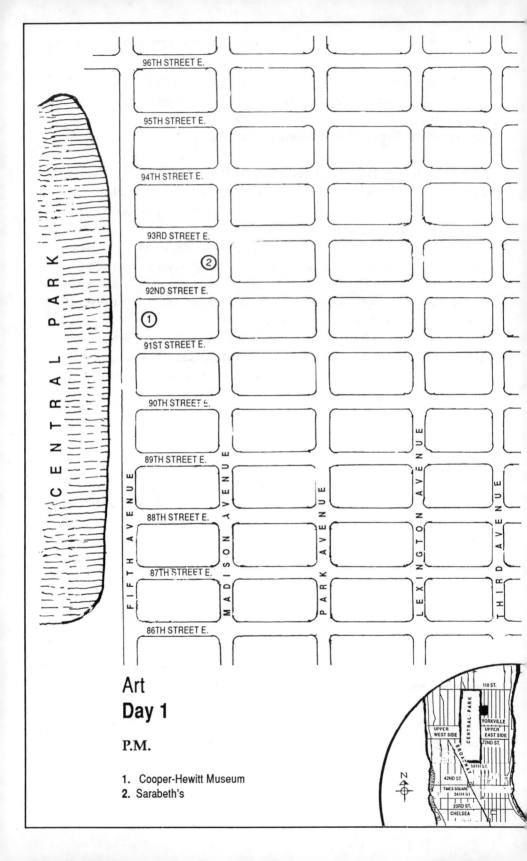

Art
Day 1

P.M.

1. Cooper-Hewitt Museum
2. Sarabeth's

Walk down the worn flight of stairs, out the front door and cross over to the benches where you can wait for the **M4** bus to take you downtown. This is about a one-half hour trip to Fifth Ave. and 86th St.

You will ride through Fort Tryon park, past the George Washington Bridge, through the Columbia University campus, turn on 110th St., past St. John's the Divine Cathedral, along the northern edge of Central Park and then south on Fifth Ave. to your departure point at 92nd St. Just pull the cord or, on the newer buses, push the plastic strip next to the window, to let the driver know you want to get off.

Noon

Walk one block east to Madison Ave. **Sarabeth's** restaurant ② is at 1295 Madison, between 92nd and 93rd Sts. Moderately priced, this is "casual American."

Afternoon

Walk to 91st St., turn right and you will be at the front door of the **Cooper-Hewitt Museum,** founded in 1897 as part ① of the Cooper Union school by the granddaughters of the 19th-century inventor/philanthropist Peter Cooper. When the tuition-free Cooper Union could no longer afford to operate the museum in 1968, it was entrusted to the Smithsonian Institution. Open Tuesday, 10 a.m. to 9 p.m., Wednesday through Saturday, 10 a.m. to 5 p.m.; Sunday, noon to 5 p.m., closed Monday. Admission.

The sixty-four room museum is located in the former home of Andrew Carnegie, the steel magnate, reputed to be the richest man in America at the turn of the century. The collection includes more than 300,000 objects spanning 3,000 years of design history from cultures around the world. On view are porcelain, textiles, silverware, furniture, drawings, woodwork, glass and all manner of beautiful objects. In addition, major decorative art special exhibitions are usually on view. During the past years, exhibitions have ranged from subway posters to drawings of monumental arches in Galveston. This is a treasure of a museum.

Evening

Return to your hotel and rest for a while. If you are going to the theater or a concert, make your dinner reservations accordingly. Again, take your choice of the hundreds of restaurants, but let me recommend one of my favorites: **Jezebel**, on the edge of the theater district. It is right on the corner of 9th Ave. and 45th St. with a very discreet sign; look for the door.

It is faux brothel decor or Louisiana lush, *whatever*, as my grandson would say. It is really overdone and fun. Southern cooking with great honey-fried chicken and yams and good service. It also has amazing restrooms.

After dinner, you can amble up to Times Square and explore all its fabulous new treasures from the **Virgin Mega Stores'** three floors to the 60 large video screens in the **All Star** sports cafe, both at the corner of Times Square and 45th St. Even though the Jumbotron has been removed, they have left enough big blinking signs to read the newspaper by at night.

You are also near many of the Broadway theatres — so the array of choices for your evening is vast.

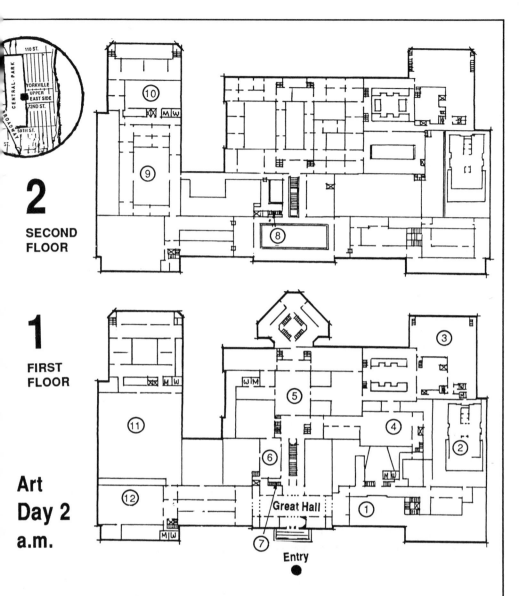

2

SECOND FLOOR

1

FIRST FLOOR

Art Day 2 a.m.

Great Hall

Entry

Metropolitan Museum of Art Floor Plan

First Floor

1. Egyptian Art
2. Temple of Dendur
3. The American Wing
4. Arms and Armor
5. Medieval Art
6. 16th-Century Spanish Patio
7. Escalator
11. Art of Africa, the Americas and Pacific Islands
12. Restaurant

Second Floor

8. Escalator
9. Impressionist/Post Impressionist Art
10. 20th-Century Art

Day 2

Highlights: The **Metropolitan Museum of Art, galleries on Madison Avenue** and the **Whitney Museum of American Art**.

Reservations: Orso for pre-theater supper, 322 W. 46th St. Try to make your reservations at least a week in advance. *Telephone 489-7212.*

Morning

Begin your day at **The Metropolitan Museum of Art**, 82nd St. and Fifth Ave., when the museum opens at 9:30 a.m. Here is an entrance! A huge stairway leading to a bank of doors, enormous banners waving in the breeze announcing major traveling exhibitions and people congregated on the steps: resting, people watching and eating pretzels from the carts parked near the curbs.

The museum is open Sunday and Tuesday through Thursday from 9:30 a.m. to 5:15 p.m.; Friday and Saturday from 9:30 a.m. to 8:45 p.m.; closed Monday.

Walk up the steps, through the doors into one of the most impressive rooms anywhere, the **Great Hall**. A circular information desk is located in the center of the lobby, where you can get advice and maps from knowledgeable and pleasant people.

To your right and left as you enter are cloakrooms where I encourage you to check (free) your coats and packages.

On the far side of the hall, beyond the information desk, are the Met's wonderful shops. On your left is the shop filled with reproductions of objects from the collections and other goods. On your right is the large bookstore.

Four huge arches always contain gorgeous floral arrangements. You can thank Lila Acheson Wallace, co-founder of *Reader's Digest* for these. She is also responsible for funding the renovated Egyptian Galleries and the Twentieth Century Galleries. The arts have rarely had a better friend. She also spear-headed the American funding for the renovation of Monet's studio, house and gardens in Giverny, France.

Pick up the newest maps; things are always changing here. I shall try to move you around this enormous museum and help you see a few of its more than 3.3 million works of art. Plan to spend the morning here. More than a few hours result in over-kill.

Walk to the far side of the **Great Hall** to pay your admission and receive your entry button. Suggested admission.

Walk to the **north end** of the Great Hall to begin your ① morning's adventure in the **Egyptian Galleries.** At the entrance to the galleries is the 5th Dynasty Tomb of Pernebi. On your right as you enter the galleries, is the Artemidora mummy; note the necklace on this 2nd-century figure and the inscription at the foot of the mummy, "Died untimely at 27. Farewell."

As you proceed through one of the first rooms, take time to look at the wonderful tempera and encaustic painted wooden faces on your left.

Just wander through these galleries, filled with wonderful ar-tifacts. Continue past the Auditorium on your left; notice there are also restrooms on your left, just beyond the auditorium.

Watch for the signs which will lead you sharply to your left into the **Sackler Wing and the Temple of Dendur.** It was a gift ② from the Egyptian government in appreciation for U.S. help in saving the monuments behind the Aswan High Dam. The temple is housed in an enormous glass domed room and sur-rounded by pools of water. It was built for two brothers who drowned in the Nile in 25 B.C. during war campaigns.

At the far end of the room, you will find a door leading into the **American Wing.** Turn sharply left, past the life-size Medea ③ sculpture, through the glass doors directly ahead of you. On your right is the American Wing Garden Court with gorgeous stained glass by Tiffany, LaFarge and Frank Lloyd Wright. On your left is the huge Vanderbilt mantelpiece with the figures of Amor and Pax by Saint-Gaudens. It will give you some idea of the size of the house from which it was taken.

Walk through the **Garden Court,** turn left to the glass doors on your right. Walk through the doors, turn hard left and walk through the red room. On your right you will pass a wonderful dark and musty bedroom from the Sagredo Palazzo in Venice. Stop a minute to admire the cherubs cavorting overhead as well as the brocade bedspread and headboard.

④ The first door on your left after the bedroom will take you to the **Arms and Armor Gallery.**

⑤ Retrace your steps to the door you entered, walk straight ahead, past the European sculpture and decorative arts on your right, until you come to the **Medieval Art** gallery on your right. There you will see the great Spanish Gate; you can just look at it from the doorway or walk in and wander around it. If you happen to be here in December, you will find the Met's extraordinary Christmas tree ensconced in front of the gate, with a fabulous Neapolitan nativity creche nestled below the decorated branches.

⑥ Walk through the room with the German stained glass, right at the first door, then left through the arch to the **Spanish courtyard** and the Blumenthal Room with its tinkling fountain.

⑦
⑧ As you leave these rooms, an immediate right will take you to the **escalator** and the second floor.

⑨ Turn left, walk along the open stairway. At the first doorway turn left, up the panelled hallway, to the **Impressionist** and
⑩ **20th Century Art Galleries.**

You will come to the **Andre Meyer** galleries filled with **Impressionist** and **Post-Impressionist** paintings, including a huge gallery filled with Degas paintings. The Turners and Courbets are on your right; and Cezanne and Degas on your left.

Turn right and walk through the galleries to the entrance of the new **20th Century Galleries** opened in the summer of 1987. Lila Acheson Wallace's foundation gave the museum the first $11 million toward this $26 million wing a few years before she died in 1984 at the age of 94. As I said earlier, her benefactions toward the arts are legendary and this is one of her greatest. The staff has begun calling this building, with 22 galleries on three floors, the "Lila Wing."

At this point during the summer months, you may first want to wander up a flight of stairs to the **roof garden** to see the sculpture and the views. The David Smith stainless steel sculpture, *Becca*, is very handsome and the views across Central Park are wonderful. Frankly, I was not impressed with most of the other sculpture, nor with the roof-top design.

But the modern galleries knocked my socks off. No matter where you start, you will have a wonderful time with the art, the great views of the park, the angled glass skylights and the balcony overlooking the first floor. On this second floor you will find Ellsworth Kelly's disorienting *Blue Panel*, Noguchi's marble, and a great Jackson Pollock, *Autumn Rhythm (#30)*.

Mark Rothko's singing canvases and Morris Louis huge color canvases are hanging near Clyfford Still's huge paintings. And I love Red Grooms' *Chance Encounter at 3 a.m.* showing Mark Rothko and William De Kooning meeting at Washington Arch.

Walk down the steps to the mezzanine, pausing to look through the windows to see the Egyptian obelisk in Central Park. The sculpture on the mezzanine is wonderful.

Since the installations of these contemporary paintings and sculptures change so rapidly, it is impossible to suggest what will be on view at your visit. Walk down steps to the first floor of this series of galleries to continue to explore. There is even a furniture and decorative arts gallery here.

Walk straight ahead through the **Michael C. Rockefeller Wing,** ⑪ filled with the **art of Africa, the Americas and the Pacific Is-**

lands. These enormous galleries (42,000 square feet) house more than 1500 objects. Note the huge Asmat canoe with the carved figures on the prow; the ritual poles; and the wonderful masks and headdresses. You will only get a brief look at this collection; just enough to lure you back another time.

Noon

As you leave the Rockefeller Wing, you will find the **museum's restaurants** on your right. You can eat in the ex- cellent cafeteria, self service, or in the restaurant in the middle of the room with waiter service. Lunch in the "sit-down" restaurant is served from 11:30 a.m. to 3:30 p.m. on Sunday and Tuesday through Thursday, 11 a.m. to 4:30 p.m., Friday and Saturday. If you want to make a reservation, call 570-3964, although it is probably not necessary. Entrees are moderate.

After lunch, re-enter the **Great Hall**: On your right is a **restored room** from a villa buried by the eruption of Mount Vesuvius in A.D. 79 near the town of Boscoreale, Italy; it was unearthed in 1900. The mosaic floor and bed are not from the original house, but from the period. This is one of the Met's masterpieces.

You may want to take a little time in the excellent shops, filled with reproductions and books. Pick up your coats and parcels and walk down the grand staircase to Fifth Ave.

Afternoon

Cross Fifth Ave. and walk one block east to Madison Ave. The largest collection of **art and antique galleries** in the city is located on Madison Ave. from 82nd to 57th Sts. and along the streets radiating east and west of Madison.

Most of these galleries are closed Sunday and Monday. Check newspapers for special exhibitions and gallery hours since they change often. Wander into any gallery which takes your fancy. You may have to ring a bell for admission; that is just for security purposes.

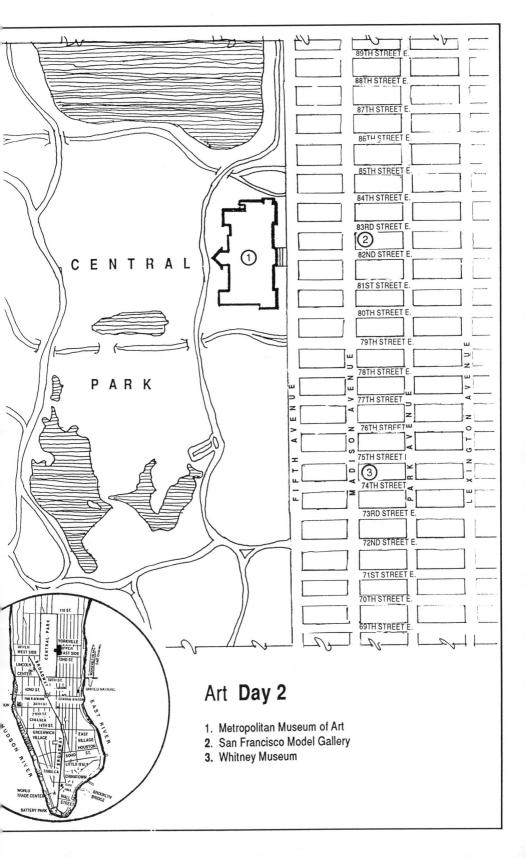

CENTRAL

PARK

89TH STREET E.
88TH STREET E.
87TH STREET E.
86TH STREET E.
85TH STREET E.
84TH STREET E.
83RD STREET E.
82ND STREET E.
81ST STREET E.
80TH STREET E.
79TH STREET E.
78TH STREET E.
77TH STREET
76TH STREET
75TH STREET
74TH STREET
73RD STREET E.
72ND STREET E.
71ST STREET E.
70TH STREET E.
69TH STREET E.

FIFTH AVENUE
MADISON AVENUE
PARK AVENUE
LEXINGTON AVENUE

Art Day 2

1. Metropolitan Museum of Art
2. San Francisco Model Gallery
3. Whitney Museum

Across the street at the corner of Madison and 82nd St. (1089 Madison) is the **San Francisco Ship Model Gallery**. This is as ② close as model ships come to being works of art. It is worth a look.

At 20 E. 79th St., you will find the **Salander-O'Reilly Gallery**. The **Graham Gallery** (1014 Madison) specializes in 19th and 20th century paintings. Take a look in at **Linda Horn's** and her marvelous antiques and decorative objects. If she is true to form, she will have a remarkably installed window.

David Findley at 77th St. handles American and European painting and sculpture.

At 980 Madison at 76th St., across from the Carlyle, is the **Gagosian Gallery** with extraordinary installations of contemporary artists' work.

Continue south on Madison to 75th St., wandering into any of the art galleries or shops selling fine jewelry.

Visit the **Whitney Museum of American Art** at the corner of ③ Madison and 75th with its excellent contemporary sculpture and paintings. Open Tuesday 1 to 8 p.m., Wednesday to Saturday, 11 a.m. to 5 p.m., Sunday 12 noon to 6 p.m. Closed Monday. It is free and open to everyone Tuesday evening from 6 to 8 p.m. Check for special exhibitions.

Marcel Breuer's concrete building of grey granite is reached by a bridge over a "moat," actually a sunken sculpture garden. It is difficult to anticipate what objects from their permanent collections will be on view at any one time.

One work of art which seems to be on permanent display is Alexander Calder's *Circus*, with its wire clowns, acrobats and performing animals. A large number of Calder mobiles and stabiles are located in the courtyard.

Visit the painting galleries. A couple of my favorite paintings are in this collection: *Brooklyn Bridge* by Joseph Stella, my choice for the best image of that magnificent structure; George Bellows's painting of the great boxers, *Dempsey and Firpo;* and Edward Hopper's *Early Sunday Morning.*

Supper

Cab to **Orso's,** 322 W. 46th St., between Eighth and Ninth Aves. Eat your pasta, pizza or other grills in its vaulted skylit backroom. Dinner costs will be moderate. Open 7 days, noon to 11:30 p.m.

You are near the **theater district.** If you feel like seeing a play this evening, you can have an early supper and walk a block or so to the theaters and buy tickets at the box office.

Except for the big hits it is usually possible to get tickets for many productions by just arriving near curtain time. In fact, many times tickets are released for sale shortly before the performance and you can often get good seats if you are willing to gamble a bit.

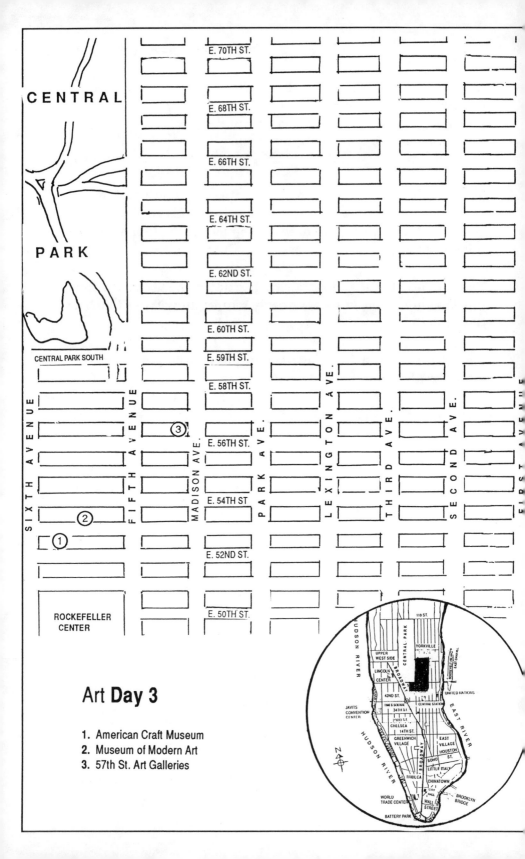

CENTRAL

PARK

CENTRAL PARK SOUTH

E. 70TH ST.

E. 68TH ST.

E. 66TH ST.

E. 64TH ST.

E. 62ND ST.

E. 60TH ST.

E. 59TH ST.

E. 58TH ST.

E. 56TH ST.

E. 54TH ST

E. 52ND ST.

E. 50TH ST.

SIXTH AVENUE

FIFTH AVENUE

MADISON AVE.

PARK AVE.

LEXINGTON AVE.

THIRD AVE.

SECOND AVE.

FIRST AVENUE

ROCKEFELLER
CENTER

Art **Day 3**

1. American Craft Museum
2. Museum of Modern Art
3. 57th St. Art Galleries

Day 3

Highlights: Museum of Modern Art, American Craft Museum and the **galleries** on 57th St.

Morning

Start your day at 10 a.m. at the new **American Craft Museum,** 53rd St., between Fifth and Sixth Avs., just across ① the street from The Museum of Modern Art. Opened more than thirty years ago in a brownstone just down the block, the new building (1986) provides four times more gallery space than the old home.

The museum is open Wednesday through Sunday, 10 a.m. to 5 p.m.; Tuesdays until 8 p.m.; closed Monday.

The building is quite extraordinary with its sweeping staircases, large windows on the main floor and excellent lighting. Children's classes are often underway on the lower level. On display may be the museum's extensive permanent collection and temporary exhibitions of such wide ranging artifacts as glass, fabrics, quilts or furniture. The permanent collections include the full range of craft media: clay, fiber, metal, wood, and glass.

Walk across the street to the **Museum of Modern Art** (MOMA), ② now complete with a residential tower looming overhead and sparkling quarters for one of the finest collections of modern art in the world. Plans are in the offing for new additions to the museum.

Open: Saturday, Sunday, Monday and Tuesday, 11 a.m. to 6 p.m.; Thursday and Friday, noon to 8:30 p.m. Closed Wednesday.

Take the escalator to the second floor and walk over to the windows on your right to look down into the sculpture garden, which you will visit at noon.

The entrance to the **Painting and Sculpture Galleries #1** is to your left as you step off the escalator. The galleries are so beautifully designed and filled with such extraordinary paintings and sculpture, you can easily find your way, but let me point out a few works you won't want to miss.

In the first room are some glorious Cezanne paintings. Rousseau's *The Sleeping Gypsy* and van Gogh's *Starry Night* as well as Toulouse Lautrec's *La Goulue at the Moulin Rouge* are on view in the Post-Impressionism galleries.

Further on are Picasso's *Les Demoiselles d'Avignon*, generally agreed to be the turning point for much of our new art. Picasso's *Harlequin* is hung near Lipchitz's sculpture, *Man with a Guitar* and as you look at them, you will recognize how they relate.

Continue through the **Expressionism** galleries, the Mondrian paintings and the Constructivist gallery, which are not my favorites. Walk on into the Matisse gallery to see his *Red Studio, Dance, Piano Lesson, Moroccans* and four bronze heads to your immediate left. Through the Kandinsky and Klee paintings to the corner gallery, filled with Picasso again. Note particularly *Night Fishing at Antibes, Girl Before a Mirror* and the 1932 plaster *Head of a Woman*.

And finally into the Miro gallery with his painting, *The Birth of the World* and through the Surrealists. Note Giacometti's skinny dog; Magritte's *The Empire of Light II*, one of my favorites; and Dali's *Petit Theatre*, a painted wood box with painted glass panes.

As you leave the painting galleries, notice the photography galleries on your left. They are filled with wonderful prints of contemporary and historical photographs as well as fine temporary exhibitions. John Szarkowski, Curator of Photography at MOMA for many years, is largely responsible, not only for this fine collection, but the acceptance of photography as a fine art in museums throughout the country.

Noon

Before you explore the rest of the museum, take the escalator down to the main floor and have lunch. **The Garden Cafe** features hot dishes, salads, sandwiches and a wide assortment of desserts and other good things. It is a pleasant place, next to the outdoor sculpture garden, one of my favorite places in town.

Wander around the **sculpture garden,** or just relax in the sun for a few minutes and enjoy being surrounded by all these treasures.

Afternoon

Take the escalator to the third floor and **Painting and Sculpture** #2 galleries. To your right are the galleries of prints and illustrated books. Directly ahead are the rooms filled with early Abstract Expressionist work and pre-World War II American art.

Note the work by Francis Bacon, particularly his frightening *Dog* with its black and red background. Walk through these galleries to reach the room with the Matisse *Swimming Pool* and *Memory of Oceania,* two of his large paper cutouts.

Then come the Abstract Expressionists. Notice particularly Jackson Pollock's *One,* a large "drip" painting; and Rothko's huge paintings. Relax a bit with Sam Francis' *Towards Disappearance II.* This should carry you through the contemporary galleries with their Pop, Op, Wham, paintings including Warhol's *Gold Marilyn,* and the works by Tony Smith and Robert Irwin.

Time to leave the museum; promise yourself you will come back. Walk west to Sixth Ave., turn right and walk north to 57th St. Between Fifth and Sixth Aves., on 57th, you can explore a ③ myriad of fine art galleries. Many of the galleries along here share the same address and most of them are located on second, third and fourth floors, easily accessible by elevator.

Don't try to visit all of these galleries; select a few which feature the type of artwork you most enjoy.

My best piece of advice in looking at galleries is to pick up the monthly *Gallery Guide*, often offered free in the galleries. It lists current exhibitions, hours, addresses and other pertinent information. You can also check exhibition listings in *New York* magazine or the *New Yorker*.

The gallery scene is changing so rapidly in New York that I will only suggest some buildings to explore that contain a number of galleries. As you walk east on 57th St., check the following: the building at 50 W. 57th; Marlborough at Number 40; the Hammer gallery at Number 33; 24 W. 57th, and Number 20 W. 57th. All these buildings have a wide variety of galleries, but change so rapidly I hesitate to list them.

At 20 West 57th, you will find the **Associated American Artists** (AAA), America's largest dealer of old and new prints, including etchings, lithographs, woodcuts and serigraphs.

On the north side of the street, notice the huge red 9 standing in front of **9 West 57th St.**, the best designed address in town.

Cross Fifth Ave., past Tiffany's and IBM with its bamboo-filled atrium, to visit a couple of other art dealers. **Pace Gallery** is at 32 East 57th and is one of the most innovative and unusual exhibition spaces. On the third floor you will find **Pace Editions** for fine prints.

At the northeast corner of 57th and Madison, Number 41 E. 57th St., is the extraordinary black-and-white Art Deco **Fuller Building.** Notice the pair of figures by Elie Nadelman over the 57th St. entrance.

Robert Miller's art gallery is located on the second floor featuring a range of media, schools and centuries of art. A number of other galleries are also in this building.

Evening

Just because you might want to have some fun this evening after all the serious art browsing, turn around on 57th St. and walk west. There are a number of "theme" restaurants along this street, some old and some brand new.

One block south of 57th on Sixth Ave. and 56th St is the **Harley Davidson Cafe**, loud and trendy. Further on is the tried and true **Hard Rock Cafe**, with surprisingly good food; **Planet Hollywood** with amazing desserts, and the **Brooklyn Diner** with excellent soups and sandwiches. Make it a moveable feast. No reservations, but you often have to wait in line. It's part of the fun.

Go on up to **Lincoln Center** and see a play, listen to a concert, go to the opera or just enjoy the space. Lots of pleasant places for drinks and coffees across the street.

City Gardens DAY 1

1. Peter Minuit Plaza
2. Admiral George Dewey Promenade
3. Bowling Green
4. Trinity Church
5. Chase Manhattan Bank
6. World Trade Center
7. Washington Market Park

8. Duane St. Park
9. St. Paul's Chapel and Churchyard
10. American Telephone & Telegraph Building
11. Woolworth Building
12. City Hall Park
13. Brooklyn Bridge
14. South Street Seaport Museum

Gardens of New York

Most people think of New York City as wall-to-wall build-ings. Of course, they know that Central Park sits right in the middle of town, but otherwise they envision walking through dark canyons of skyscrapers. The fact is the city is honeycombed with open spaces: plazas, vest-pocket parks, promenades, atriums and gardens. It's filled with lovely, and often unknown, city gardens — sometimes in surprising spots.

City planners responded to the needs of people crowded onto this small island by providing breathing room in dozens of creative ways. Developers were offered financial and space in-centives, the park board and philanthropic individuals created little vest-pocket parks and huge promenades, and private citizens found little places to plant flowers, vegetables and green plants. The city owes much of its sanity to these safety valves, planned, built and maintained all over town.

Some of these places are the best-kept secrets in Manhattan and for good reason. The neighborhoods like to think of these green oases as their secret gardens. This is your chance to discover the jewels in the city's crown and share the pleasure and beauty of these enchanting spaces.

Day I

Highlights: Battery Park, Trinity Cemetery, Chase Manhattan Plaza, St. Paul's Chapel, City Hall Park and Police Plaza.

Reservations: Lunch at **Greenhouse Cafe** in Marriott International Hotel, World Trade Center. *Telephone 444-4010.* Dinner: **The River Cafe,** 1 Water St. (at Brooklyn Bridge), Brooklyn Heights. Reservations are accepted two weeks in advance. *Telephone (718) 522-5200.* Or **Gianni's,** 15 Fulton St., South St. Seaport. *Telephone 608-7300.*

Morning

① Begin your day at the **Battery**, southernmost point of Manhattan. The subway exit is at **Peter Minuit Plaza,** named for the first governor of New Amsterdam who is reputed to have bought the island from the Indians in 1626 for $24 worth of trinkets.

② The plaza is the site of the memorial to the first Jewish immigrants to New York City. Walk south toward the harbor and Battery Park. The **Admiral George Dewey Promenade**, with its spectacular view of the harbor, is your goal. As you walk along the promenade you can see the Statue of Liberty, Ellis Island and the New Jersey coastline in the distance. On your right are a series of memorials and statues beautifully situated in the surrounding park. Since your aim today is to enjoy the open spaces of the city, this is a lovely starting place.

③ Continue walking along the promenade until you reach **Bowling Green,** the city's first park. The green was renovated during the 1970s; at the same time the adjacent street was paved with Belgian blocks. Notice the new fountain on this green space where the Dutch burghers bowled on pleasant summer evenings.

④ Walk north on Broadway for two or three blocks to **Trinity Church** and its adjoining cemetery. Here lie Robert Fulton, inventor of the steamboat; Alexander Hamilton, the first

Secretary of the Treasury, and Captain James Lawrence, who refused to give up the ship. Although this is a cemetery, it is a pretty green space. Notice the street lamp in front of Trinity, the Bishop's Crook Lamp, named for its shape.

Walk one block east on Pine St. to the **Chase Manhattan Bank** ⑤ **Plaza.** This is a huge plaza containing a sunken Japanese garden by Isamu Noguchi, with 45 pipes spraying water in various undulating patterns. The star of the plaza is the 43-foot, 25-ton sculpture by Jean Dubuffet, *Group of Four Trees*. This huge, colorful, playful construction can be walked through, under and around. I love this sculpture, even though I think it is a strange piece for a bank to commission.

Lunch

Walk back to Broadway, turn right to Liberty St., turn left to the **World Trade Center**. The **Marriott Hotel** is to the west ⑥ of Two World Trade Center, but accessible from the trade center lobby. The **Greenhouse Cafe** is in the Marriott Hotel. Lunch today will be in the most garden-like restaurant in this part of town. The glass-enclosed room allows you to see the trade center soaring above you. This is a charming room with pretty pink tablecloths, rattan chairs, plantings and tiny sparkling lights in the trees. Enjoy the good salads, omelets or sandwiches featured on its moderately priced menu. You can also order wine by the glass from an excellent wine list. Lunch is served daily from 11:30 a.m. to 3:30 p.m.

Afternoon

After lunch wander out on the Trade Center plaza to enjoy the huge space and see the sculptures. At the far west side of the North Tower is Alexander Calder's 25-ton stabile, *Three Red Wings*.

There are two parks just four or five blocks north of the World Trade Center. If you are feeling energetic, I suggest you walk up to see them. Otherwise, resume your tour at this spot when you return from this side excursion.

Walk north on West Broadway about four blocks to Chamber
⑦ St. The block-square **Washington Market Park** is located between Chambers and Reade Sts., on Greenwich St. It was built
on a vacant lot by the city's Department of Housing Preservation and Development and a number of community groups.
The large lawn encompasses a playground, a gazebo-
bandstand, winding paths, roses and comfortable seating from
which to enjoy the fine view of Battery Park City Towers. A
cast-iron fence adds the final touch to this very special park. It
is located next to Manhattan Community College. Notice the
fine sculpture of *Icarus* by Roy Shifrin at the top of the steps
leading from the park to the campus.

Head one block east on Duane St. and you will come to the
⑧ oldest park in New York, a tiny triangle called **Duane Park** at
the intersection of Duane and Hudson Sts. After I was there, I
decided not to mention it since it was in such disastrous condition. But it is scheduled for a face-lift. Plans are underway to install ornate cast-iron street lamps and fencing, to plant ivy,
grass and shrubs, and to install decorative paving and a pedestal for sculpture. In 1797 the city bought the property from
Trinity Church for $5. I suspect they are going to spend a bit
more for the renovation. Incidentally, notice the fine 19th-cen-
tury buildings which surround the park. You will have to look
above the first floors since the buildings now seem to house the
butter and cheese industry in New York.

Walk south on West Broadway back to our afternoon starting
⑨ point at Vesey St. Turn east on Vesey, a block or so to **St. Paul's
Chapel and Churchyard**, the oldest church in town. George
Washington may not have slept here, but he worshiped here;
his pew is still marked. Wander around the churchyard with its
burial plots for some lesser-known actors, lawyers and
patriots.

Just south of St. Paul's, at the corner of Broadway and Fulton
⑩ Sts., is the **American Telephone and Telegraph Building** with
more columns than any other building anywhere. It has eight
tiers of Ionic columns and one tier of Doric columns.

Walk north on Broadway, past the **Woolworth Building**. On ⑪
second thought, you cannot walk past the Woolworth Building.
Its beautiful interior is one of New York's great urban spaces.
So go inside and marvel at the golden marbled walls, vaulted
ceilings, murals and the grand marble staircase.

Across the street is **City Hall Park**, once a cow pasture and now ⑫
as close to a town green as this city possesses. Statues of
Nathan Hale ("I regret that I have but one life to lose for my
country.") and Horace Greeley, the famous newspaper man
("Go West, young man, go west") can be found amid the
flowering trees and fountain. The park sets off the architectural
jewel that is New York's City Hall. Fortunately, it has been restored to much of its original splendor.

Finally this afternoon, take the most important and beautiful
walk in the city, the mile-long trip across the **Brooklyn Bridge**. ⑬
Or, you can walk out to the middle of the bridge and return.
This is the only bridge with an elevated promenade for walkers
and bikers. The walk will take about 30 minutes each way,
depending on how many times you stop to savor the views.

The **entrance** to the wooden walkway is to the east of City Hall.
This is the bridge painted by Georgia O'Keeffe, John Marin and
Joseph Stella; written about by Thomas Wolfe, Hart Crane and
Walt Whitman; and jumped off by Steve Brodie, so the legend
goes. P.T. Barnum walked 21 elephants across in 1884 to prove
its stability and, not incidentally, to generate publicity for his
entertainments.

The bridge with its soaring cables may be the most beautiful
structure in New York, and its view of the river, the harbor and
the city is undeniably the finest. Stand in the middle of the
bridge and listen to the singing of the cables; take hold of them
to feel the movement. This is THE urban space in New York.

If you choose to walk across the bridge to Brooklyn, plan to eat
at the very expensive **River Cafe** at the foot of the bridge. This
anchored barge serves excellent American food, using the
finest American produce, seafood, poultry and meats. Service

is from 6:30 to 11 p.m., Sunday through Thursday; 7 to 11:30 p.m. Friday and Saturday. The cafe accepts reservations two weeks in advance. You will enjoy marvelous views of the harbor and city as you eat your elegant dinner. After dinner, cab back to your hotel.

Or, if you decided to return to Manhattan, go to the **South Street Seaport Museum.** Retrace your steps past City Hall, cross Park Row, turn left a short block and right on Nassau St., a pedestrian walkway, then past a lot of rather unattractive discount-type stores. Walk about three blocks to Fulton St., turn left and proceed to the seaport.

There are many choices for dinner as you explore this wonderful urban space. One I suggest is **Gianni's** at 15 Fulton St. If the weather is nice, eat at their outdoor cafe; if not dine on the first floor rather than the more expensive second floor.

Day 2

Highlights: International Paper Plaza, McGraw Hill and Exxon plazas, Rockefeller Center, Museum of Modern Art Sculpture Garden, Paley Park, Trump Tower, the Grand Army Plaza, Central Park and Lincoln Center.

Reservations: Dinner at **Tavern on the Green.** Central Park W. and 67th St. *Telephone 873-3200.* Or supper at **Opera Espresso.** 1928 Broadway at 65th St. *Telephone 799-3050.* Or **Lincoln Square Coffee Shoppe.** Lincoln Square between 65th and 66th Sts. *Telephone 799-4000.* Or **The Saloon.** 1920 Broadway at 64th St. *Telephone 874-1500.*

Get tickets for an evening theater, opera, music or dance production at Lincoln Center, if you can.

After the theater at **Cafe La Fortuna.** 69 W. 71st St. between Columbus and Central Park W. *Telephone 724-5846.* Or **Eclair's.** 141 W. 72nd between Columbus and Amsterdam. *Telephone 873-7700.*

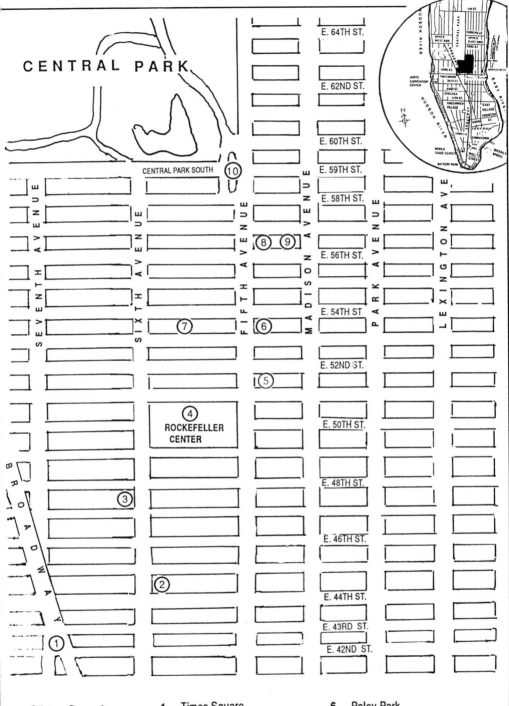

CENTRAL PARK

CENTRAL PARK SOUTH

E. 64TH ST.
E. 62ND ST.
E. 60TH ST.
E. 59TH ST.
E. 58TH ST.
E. 56TH ST.
E. 54TH ST
E. 52ND ST.
E. 50TH ST.
E. 48TH ST.
E. 46TH ST.
E. 44TH ST.
E. 43RD ST.
E. 42ND ST.

SEVENTH AVENUE
SIXTH AVENUE
FIFTH AVENUE
MADISON AVENUE
PARK AVENUE
LEXINGTON AVE.
BROADWAY

④ ROCKEFELLER CENTER

City Gardens
Day 2
a.m.

1. Times Square
2. International Paper Plaza
3. McGraw Hill Plaza
4. Rockefeller Plaza
5. Olympic Tower
6. Paley Park
7. Museum of Modern Art
8. Trump Tower
9. Sony
10. Grand Army Plaza

Morning

① Start the day about 10 a.m. at **Times Square**, 42nd St. and Broadway. The heart of the city, this may be the noisiest and most congested square in Manhattan, but it is also the most famous and exciting, in spite of its pornography, shooting galleries and hustlers. It is also the center of New York's theater district, good restaurants and two hundred miles of neon tubing. You will return here the evening of your third day to see all this neon lighted, but it is also very special in the daylight hours.

Walk into the center of the confluence of Broadway and Seventh Ave. to Father Duffy Square, where a statue of the World War I hero and pastor stands facing the back of the statue of the entertainer George M. Cohan, our Yankee Doodle Dandy. This is a good vantage point from which to examine this extraordinary open space. On a nice day, more sun pours into this square than almost any place else in the city, partly due to the numbers of four and five-story buildings surrounding the space. Don't spend too much time here; just enough to get a feeling for it.

② Walk east to Sixth Ave. and north to 45th St. and the **International Paper Plaza**, located behind the Tower at Number 1166. The garden features low brick walls, a fountain and sculpture. Shade, quiet, water, comfortable seating and breezes make this one of the most pleasant spots in mid-town Manhattan.

③ Just a few blocks north, on Sixth Ave. between 47th and 48th Sts., is **McGraw Hill's** sunken plaza with reflecting pool, honey locust trees, and abstract sculpture; the pavement is slippery when wet. West of the building is a small park with a waterfall and tunnel. The **Exxon Building plaza** at 49th St. fills the block with its plaza and fountain.

One block west on 50th St., between Sixth and Seventh Avs., near Radio City Music Hall is a charming little park. Its white chairs and tables surround a fountain.

Walk east on 50th St. to **Rockefeller Plaza** on your right. In the ④
winter this is home to the city's famous ice skating rink; in the
summer the plaza is surrounded by outdoor cafes.

Walk east through the Channel Gardens, leading to Fifth Ave.
Each season they are planted and decorated accordingly, with
Easter lilies in the spring and Christmas angels in December.
My favorites are the topiary trees, pruned in the shape of exotic
animals, which are often in the gardens in the summer. Inciden-
tally, they are called Channel Gardens because they, like the
English Channel, separate the British and French buildings lo-
cated on either side.

Walk into the **International Building** on Fifth Ave., directly
across from St. Patrick's Cathedral. A huge sculpture of Atlas is
in front. Notice the gold leaf ceiling, gold abstract sculptural
details and bust of Charles Lindbergh at the head of the escalator.

Cross Fifth Ave. to **Olympic Tower** at 51st St. This through- ⑤
block arcade features a three-story waterfall, which cascades
into a lighted pool. The tower is open from 8 a.m. to 6 p.m.
weekdays and from 9 a.m. to 6 p.m. on Saturday.

Continue north on Fifth Ave. to 53rd St. Turn right on 53rd St.,
a few steps, to the vest-pocket **Paley Park**. Built on the former ⑥
site of the famous Stork Club, this charming place draws you
up its two or three steps toward sheltering trees, tiny tables and
the sparkling wall of water at the far end of the space, if this
tiny park can be said to have a far end. You can rest, get a cup
of coffee at the snack bar and just enjoy this oasis located smack
dab in the middle of town.

Return to Fifth Ave. and continue west on 53rd half a block to ⑦
the **Museum of Modern Art** to view its remarkable sculpture
garden. The museum is open Saturday through Tuesday from
11 a.m. to 6 p.m.; Thursday and Friday, 12 noon to 8:30 p.m.
Closed on Wednesday. Admission.

Noon

Lunch in the Modern's **Garden Cafe,** near the sculpture garden, is a very pleasant experience. The cafe is open Friday through Tuesday, 11 a.m. to 5 p.m., Thursday 12 noon to 7:45 p.m., closed Wednesday. There are three separate lines for food in this pleasant cafeteria: hot dishes, pastry, fruit and desserts, and soup, salad and sandwiches. Prices are moderate.

A second floor restaurant, **Sette MOMA,** overlooks the sculpture garden. Pricey pasta, but pleasant.

After lunch, wander through the garden and sculpture by Picasso, Renoir, Miro, Rodin and others. You do not have time to see much of the museum on this tour (See Art Lover's New York), but do take the time to escalate to the second floor to see the one room filled with the Monet water lily paintings.

Afternoon

⑧ Walk back to Fifth Ave., turn left and continue to 56th St. and the 68-story **Trump Tower** across the street. Enter past the liveried doormen and limousines, around the grand piano (which may be in use) toward the waterfall streaming down the apricot-colored, marbled walls, which soar six floors high. This extravagant building houses multi-million dollar condominiums, office spaces and some of the most expensive shops in the city.

⑨ Around the corner is the **Sony Building** and its Atrium at 56th St. and Madison Ave. Somehow I always feel this is one of the stranger spaces in town. It is filled with soaring bamboo which seem to almost touch the skylight and reflect on the surrounding glass walls. There are a number of small tables and chairs to which you can carry your trays from the nearby pastry and coffee kiosk. Open 10 a.m. to 10 p.m., every day.

⑩ Head back to Fifth Ave., then right to 59th St. and the **Grand Army Plaza,** location of the Plaza Hotel, the horse drawn carriages, and the entrance to Central Park. Note the Pulitzer

Fountain adorned with the statue of Abundance. This huge square is one of the city's treasures, as well as being one of the coolest spots in summer.

Plan to spend the afternoon exploring **Central Park**. If you want to visit the park in a horse and buggy, this is the time to decide. You can rent a rig for about $34 for a half-hour, but for longer rides you can negotiate your rate before getting aboard. This can be a very pleasant way to see parts of this enormous 840-acre park.

If you want to strike out on foot, follow me. The poet, William Cullen Bryant, helped launch Central Park in 1850, through a campaign in his paper, The New York Post. The city acquired the land, then a swamp, and awarded the design contract to Frederick Law Olmsted and Calvert Vaux. This man-made landscape was carved out of bogs, cliffs, glacial deposits and pig farms. The south end of the park is meandering, serene and more formal; the north end is rougher, grander and tougher.

It took 15 years to build the park; 40 years for the plantings to grow. Note particularly the hundreds of types of evergreens, flowers and shrubs; the sunken roads which permit travel across the park without interfering with the pedestrian and bike travel; the wonderful bridges and arches throughout the park; the extravagant placement of sculpture, exotic gazebos and other structures; and the more recent advent of concrete spaces for recreational activity. The Central Park Conservancy is now busy rebuilding and replacing some of the former grandeur of the park, which was lost due to over-use and neglect.

The park is officially open until midnight, but stay out of it after dark. It is closed to motorized traffic on weekends.

Enter the park at the corner of 59th St. and Fifth Ave. **The Pond** ①
is to your left where you can feed the already overfed ducks with crumbs from the pretzel you can buy from the nearby vendor.

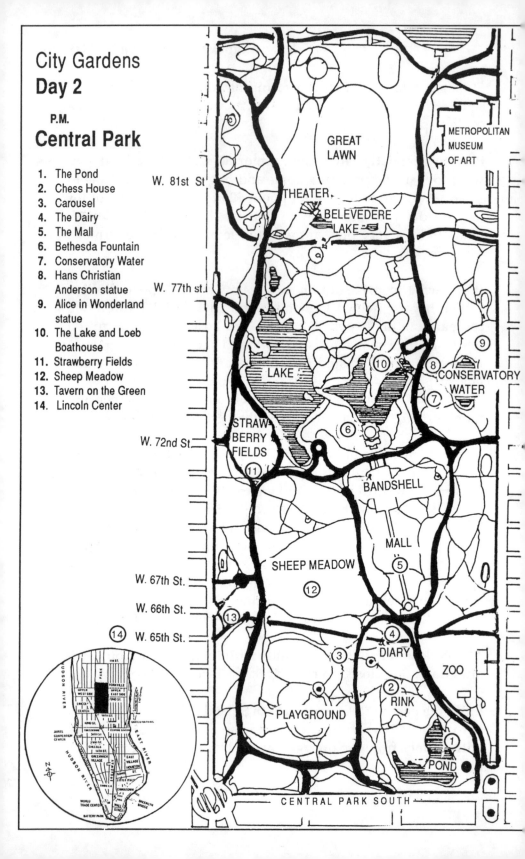

City Gardens
Day 2

P.M.
Central Park

1. The Pond
2. Chess House
3. Carousel
4. The Dairy
5. The Mall
6. Bethesda Fountain
7. Conservatory Water
8. Hans Christian Anderson statue
9. Alice in Wonderland statue
10. The Lake and Loeb Boathouse
11. Strawberry Fields
12. Sheep Meadow
13. Tavern on the Green
14. Lincoln Center

METROPOLITAN MUSEUM OF ART

GREAT LAWN

THEATER
BELEVEDERE LAKE

W. 81st St

W. 77th st.

CONSERVATORY WATER

LAKE

STRAW BERRY FIELDS

W. 72nd St.

BANDSHELL

MALL

SHEEP MEADOW

W. 67th St.
W. 66th St.
W. 65th St.

DIARY

ZOO

RINK

PLAYGROUND

POND

CENTRAL PARK SOUTH

Walk along the bank, past **Wollman Rink**, built by the developer Donald Trump in a matter of months, after the city had delayed construction for years. Filled with ice skaters in the winter, it sometimes features concerts or other divertissements in the summer.
day 2 p.m.

Just north of the rink and up a flight of steps, is the red and yellow brick **Chess House**, filled with people playing on the built- ②
in chess boards; you need to bring your own chess men. The house was restored with funds from the financier Bernard Baruch who maintained an 'office' on a bench in Central Park. Incidentally, there are fairly clean and comfortable rest rooms located here.

Walk down the steps on the far side. A **Victorian carousel** is ③
just across the road. Admission. You can ride the merry-go-round with its wonderful collection of 58 old-fashioned hand-carved horses. The largest horses are three-quarters the size of real horses and are the most ornately designed.

Recross the road and walk east to **The Dairy**, now the park's in- ④
formation center. In 1870, milkmaids used to dispense milk to mothers and children just as the name implies. The house has been rebuilt to the original drawings and painted Victorian colors. The last time I was there they were hanging lanterns, huge white satin bows and flowers in preparation for a wedding. You can pick up current maps, get information about the day's activities and watch a short slide show about the park. It is closed Monday.

Cross the 65th St. Transverse and proceed north to the **Mall,** ⑤
leading to the Bethesda Terrace and Fountain. The Mall is a long, formal promenade flanked by double rows of American elms. This was one of the first and most redesigned features in the park. Notice the sculpture as you go down this long, rather dark broad walk. At the end of the Mall you will emerge into the light with the Naumburg Bandshell on your right, now being replaced. Beyond the bandshell is the Wisteria Pergola, also being re-arranged.

⑥ Walk through the underpass where the original ceiling tiles were reinstalled and you will emerge in front of the **Bethesda Fountain**.

⑦ Climb the stairs and turn left on the 72nd St. Transverse to the first main walkway. On your left is the **Conservatory Water** where large and small children sail their model boats. A bronze ⑧ **Hans Christian Andersen and his Ugly Duckling** sit at the side of the water waiting for storytellers in the summer. At the far end of the pond is a wonderful sculpture of **Alice in** ⑨ **Wonderland** and her friends, including the Mad Hatter. This is one of my favorite spots in the park. I love this sculpture which is rubbed smooth and shiny from the children who climb up to sit on Alice's lap.

⑩ Just west of the pond is **The Lake and the Loeb Boathouse** where you can rent rowboats or take a ride in a real Venetian gondola. The bike rentals are also located here. The Boathouse Snack Bar will provide you with food and drink.

This is as far north as this afternoon's tour goes. You will actually have explored only the lower third of the park, and just barely touched that section.

⑪ Return to the 72nd St. Transverse, walk west and you will pass **Strawberry Fields** on your right. This is the area reconstructed with a gift from Yoko Ono, John Lennon's widow. He and his family lived in the Dakota apartments, just across West Central Park. It was in front of this building that he was killed in 1980. This memorial bears the name of one of his musical hits, *Strawberry Fields Forever*. This is one of the loveliest, most serene areas in the park, with cobblestone paths, beautiful trees and shrubs. A resting place with benches is located just off Central Park West and 72nd St. Notice the starburst marble mosaic on the ground in the middle of this little open space. It carries the single word, *Imagine*, the title of a song by Lennon. It was a gift from the city of Naples, Italy and is based on an ancient Pompeiian mosaic.

Walk south, past **Sheep Meadow** on your left, site of the park's park's famous outdoor opera, Philharmonic and rock concerts.

Evening

At the 65th St. Transverse, you will come to the fine restaurant, **Tavern on the Green**, on your right. I cannot think ⑬ of a more fitting end to this day of exploring the urban landscape. The glass enclosed room with its Baccarat chandeliers, the multi-colored ceiling, the attentive service and lovely food always make me feel a bit like Cinderella at the ball. The restaurant is a glorious stage set and you are the star. It is a tourist favorite, but for a very good reason: it is wonderful. Expensive, but wonderful. It also has Patrick Clark for its chef, which has made its food as spectacular as its decor.

An inside New York tip: Tavern on the Green's new Chestnut Room is one of the city's best bargains. On Wednesday night they charge a $5 cover to listen to some of the best entertainment in town. Obviously, you can order food and drinks in addition, but be certain to make reservations. It is becoming very popular.

If you want something less expensive, walk west on 65th St. to **Lincoln Center**. Several inexpensive restaurants are in this ⑭ area: **The Opera Espresso** at 1928 Broadway at 65th St., an elegant coffee shop with good sandwiches, omelets and hamburgers; the **Lincoln Square Coffee Shop** on Lincoln Square, between 65th and 66th Sts., for a very good salad bar, good soups and all kinds of sandwiches; and **The Saloon** at 1920 Broadway and 64th St. for good salads, sandwiches and lots of daily specials.

At any event, wherever you eat, plan to explore the gorgeous Lincoln Center consortium of theatres, the Avery Fisher Hall for music, and the Metropolitan Opera House. Explore the plazas, particularly the one between the Opera house and the Vivian Beaumont and Mitzi E. Newhouse theaters with its reflecting pool and two-piece bronze work by Henry Moore. A Calder sculpture is located near the entrance to the library.

With luck, you were able to reserve a ticket for an opera, ballet, concert or theater production so you can see the interior of at least one of these magnificent buildings. I have still not recovered from my first visit to the Metropolitan Opera, with its glorious grand staircase, the Chagall murals and 3,788-seat auditorium which seemed totally lined in red. Still bright and shining in my memory is the moment when the lights dimmed, the magnificent chandelier seemed to vanish in the ceiling, and the orchestra began the overture.

After your evening entertainment, walk north on Columbus Ave. for an espresso and pastry at **Cafe La Fortuna**, 69 W. 71st St., between Columbus and Central Park West. Or try the back room of **Eclair's** (in business for more than 50 years) at 141 W. 72nd St., between Columbus and Amsterdam Aves., for a Viennese torte or eclair and coffee with whipped cream.

And off to bed. One day remains in which to explore a few more open spaces in this city of innumerable choices.

Day 3

Highlights: Ford Foundation, United Nations Gardens, Amster Yard, Plazas and Atriums, Citicorp Center, Park Avenue, and Times Square at night.

Reservations: Oyster Bar at Grand Central Station for pre-theater appetizers. *Telephone 490-6650.* Reserve theater tickets. Reservations for supper after theater in the **Algonquin Hotel** lobby. 59 W. 44th St. *Telephone 840-6800.*

Morning

① Start the day on **42nd St.**, just south of **Grand Central Station.** You will make a complete circle today and return to Grand Central and its famous Oyster Bar and a look at its grand interior later this afternoon. You are going to visit several indoor atriums, those glass-enclosed public spaces which have been included in many of the structures built in New York in the last 25 years.

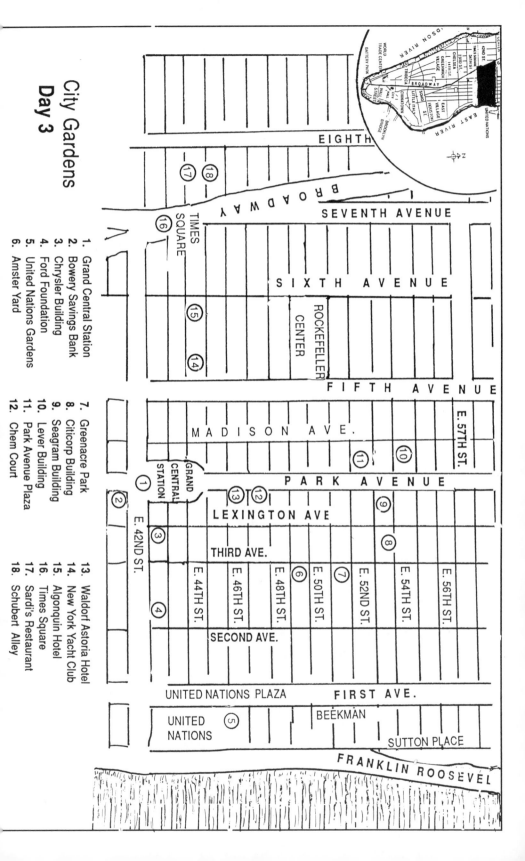

City Gardens
Day 3

1. Grand Central Station
2. Bowery Savings Bank
3. Chrysler Building
4. Ford Foundation
5. United Nations Gardens
6. Amster Yard

7. Greenacre Park
8. Citicorp Building
9. Seagram Building
10. Lever Building
11. Park Avenue Plaza
12. Chem Court

13. Waldorf Astoria Hotel
14. New York Yacht Club
15. Algonquin Hotel
16. Times Square
17. Sardi's Restaurant
18. Schubert Alley

The collection of tall glass boxes built in the 1950s and 60s began to give the city a kind of sterile quality. The movers and shakers determined that through zoning incentives, they could encourage architects and developers to add amenities to their plans. Today it is unusual not to find plazas, pools, shops and restaurants in these enclosed spaces.

I am from Minneapolis, the home of the glass-enclosed skyway system, where you can walk throughout the downtown city, from building to building, without ever setting foot outdoors. An enclosed 'second city' above the streets makes a considerable amount of sense, given this northern city's lengthy cold and snowy winters and hot, humid summers. However, I find it strange to see this development in New York City. Its noisy, crowded, bustling streets, filled with people who all seem to know exactly where they are going, gives New York its energy and excitement. Moving that life into these enclaves of glass and espresso bars seems a strange undertaking to me. Visit some of these spots today and make up your own mind.

(2) Begin at the corner of Park Ave. and 42nd St. **The Bowery Savings** Bank is at 110 E. 42nd St. Built in 1923, its monumental main room features marble columns, a beamed ceiling 65 feet high, a mosaic floor and incredible ornate brass tables with fancy little lamps to illumine your check writing. Note the animals carved overhead on the columns: squirrels for thrift and bears and bulls for Wall Street. Step into the side room to see the stenciled ceiling and tapestries by A. Refregier extolling the virtues of planting, reaping, family, peace and the arts.

Across the street is the 1980 **Grand Hyatt Hotel**. Its four-story atrium is filled with fountains, plants and a huge sculpture.

Cross the street for a quick look into the lobby of the great (3) **Chrysler Building,** 135 42nd St., one of the city's most beautiful. Check the marbled walls, recessed lighting, inlaid elevator doors, overhead mural and Art Deco details.

Between Second and Third Aves. is the **New York Daily News Building**. Step inside to see the enormous globe slowly revolving in the space between the first floor and the lower level of the building.

Continue east on 42nd St. to the **Ford Foundation,** between (4) Second and Third Aves. It is open Monday to Friday from 9 a.m. to 5 p.m. This was the first (1964) and the best of the dozens of atriums which would proliferate throughout town. Its lavish interior gardens and pool set the standard for all the copies to come, some of which you will see later today. It certainly did not hurt to have the funds to build and decorate this space so beautifully.

Go half a block further east and you will be in front of the **United Nations** headquarters. Today you are not going to enter (5) the building (you can do that on another tour), but you are going to walk through some of the gardens.

Turn left and walk north on the United Nations Plaza to 43rd St. On the west side of the street is the Ralph J. Bunche Park, with its sculpture honoring the Nobel Peace Prize winner.

Continue north on the Plaza to the 46th St. Visitor's Entrance, open from 9 a.m. to 5 p.m. This is also the entrance to the **U.N. Public Gardens** with their rose gardens, sculpture and view of the East River. Walk along the promenade, past the manicured lawn and hedges on the east end of the park. Look particularly for the memorial to Eleanor Roosevelt with its stone seat and pink marble containing the words: "She would rather light a candle than curse the darkness and her glow has warmed the world."

As you leave the park, walk west on **Dag Hammerskjold Plaza,** an extension of 47th St. This area is being renovated.

Turn right on Second Ave., walk north to 49th St., turn left. Between Second and Third Aves., you will find the **Turtle Bay Gardens Historic District** with two rows of ten houses, back to back. A common garden serves all the buildings, although it is impossible to tell that from the streetside.

⑥ Across the street is **Amster Yard #211**, renovated carriage houses built around a garden court. If the gate is open, as it was on my last trip, you can enter through an arcade from 49th St. and walk over the slate floor to see the garden's wrought iron furniture, ivy-covered walls, flowers, trees and strange large mirror which reflects back the entire garden. The gate is often locked so it is just luck if you get in to see this pretty place.

Walk out to Third Avenue and turn right. Between 50th and 51st Sts. you will find **Ess-A-Bagel.** This is the perfect time to rest your feet, have a coffee and taste a real New York bagel. In almost every story which chased the best bagel in the city, Ess-A-Bagel won. Theirs are big and chewy and fantastic. And you can have everything from plain to garlic to cinnamon-raison to onion to oat bran and a dozen kinds of cream cheeses. Do try the Gaspe salmon, which "Uncle Bill" will slice for you. Try it; I think you'll like it.

⑦ Walk north to 51st St. A few steps to your right is **Greenacre Park**, one of New York's loveliest three-level vest-pocket parks. A 25-foot-high waterfall is set into the rear wall's lowest level. A brook runs from the sidewalk entrance, along the east wall, to the waterfall. The patio is paved with brick; honey locust trees and a trellis roof provide shade. A snack bar is located near the entrance to the park, which, incidentally, provides excellent food. The water sounds mask the traffic noise; the green plants and trees provide shelter from the swirling activity of the city. It is a perfect place to rest your feet and lift your spirits.

⑧ Back to Third Ave., two blocks north to 53rd St., turn left to Lexington and the **Citicorp Building.** It is one of the most recognizable on the New York skyline with 59 stories and a slanted roofline. Originally the plan was to build terraced penthouse apartments; these were not approved by the city planning board. Later attempts to install a solar energy system with panels on the roof were not successful either, but the roof design was never altered.

Lunch

Enter the lower level to visit the **Atrium** with its skylight towering above seven stories of shops and restaurants. Take your pick of the restaurants here.

Afternoon

Visit **Saint Peter's Church** which occupies a corner of Citicorp. Take time to step into the Erol Beaker Chapel, created by Louise Nevelson, New York sculptor. The natural woods are highlighted by the bright pink-and-blue patterned covers on the seats.

Leave Citicorp and walk one block west on 53rd St. to Park Ave. Take time to admire this boulevard and the beautifully landscaped area which separates the traffic. This is one of the handsomest streets in town.

On the east side of Park Ave., on your left, is the **Seagram** ⑨ **Building** (1958). Here is one of the most successful of the glass boxes on a plaza, set back 90 feet from the building line. It was the triumph of this building that induced the zoning commission to revise its code, encouraging such plazas and atriums in future building plans. Mies van der Rohe and Philip Johnson are responsible for this architecture. One of New York's finest and most expensive restaurants, The Four Seasons, is located here. Philip Johnson designed its interior, aided by a huge backdrop by Picasso, which you can see from the plaza.

Diagonally across Park Ave. is **Lever House** (1952), the first ⑩ major steel and glass building in a field of sold masonry. It does not seem so revolutionary today, but at the time it was a pioneer. Take a look at its open courtyard and garden. Its lack of seating and sun are counterbalanced by its regularly held exhibitions of art and sculpture.

Walk across the street to the **Park Avenue Plaza,** located be- ⑪ tween 52nd and 53rd Sts. It is open from 8 a.m. to 10 p.m. seven days a week. The atrium is filled with light from its glass walls on two sides and the overhead skylight. Notice the black wall of water. Look for the shops with their pretty designs. Cafe Marguery serves food but anyone can sit at their round tables with or without ordering. Marble walls surround the central elevator complex.

⑫ Walk through the atrium to 54th St., turn left to Park and right to the **Chemcourt Plaza** at 47th St.; no food, but lovely planting surrounding the nine marble waterfalls. Notice Seward Johnson's bronze sculpture, Taxi. This 1983 building for Chemical Bank is open 24 hours a day, seven days a week.

As I continued down Park Ave. one day I realized I had never been in **St. Batholomew's Church**, which is just beyond the Chemcourt Plaza. I entered through the ornate carved portico and stayed to admire the ceiling mosaics, the stained glass and the altar mural.

Walk to the altar, where you can look up to see the extravagant dome overhead and the stunning rose window on the right. Explore the side chapels on both sides of the church and especially the lovely garden on the right. This garden was almost lost in a fight some years ago over air-rights next to the church. I think you will be glad the garden won.

⑬ The **Waldorf Astoria Hotel** is just next door. Take time to walk into the reception areas and lobby of the hotel to see the newly restored Art Deco interior. $140 million can buy a lot of restoration. Particularly notice the gorgeous mosaic floor by Louis Rigal, called the *Wheel of Life*. Rigal's 13 murals depicting earthly pleasures decorate the surrounding walls. The Main Lobby features mahogany panels, a specially designed rose and green rug and a molded frieze just below the ceiling. The bronze clock in the center of the room is from the old, old Waldorf. It is all a sight to behold.

All afternoon, as you have been moving south on Park Ave., you have been seeing the Pan Am Building looming over the Helmsley Building with Grand Central Station in the background. I am not going to write the history of how this building came to be; suffice it to say, it was controversial when it was built and remains a topic of conversation about architectural integrity.

Cross 46th St., follow straight ahead on Helmsley Walk, through the Pan Am Building and suddenly you are at the head of an escalator which will bring you onto the main floor of **Grand Central Station.** An old radio series, with Grand Central Station as its locale, used to introduce each episode by announcing, "Grand Central Station, crossroads of a million private lives, gigantic stage on which are played a thousand dramas daily." The grand concourse is larger than the nave of Notre Dame in Paris.

In the spring of 1996, a $175 million, two-year restoration project was begun in this space. The star constellations and zodiac signs which decorate the enormous ceiling are being cleaned and repainted. In addition, there will be a second grand staircase, four restaurants on the balconies and shops along the concourse. At this point, no one is betting when this major effort will be completed. The terminal will continue to operate and I suspect there will be temporary shops and eating places located there during the renovation.

We will hope the famous **Grand Central Oyster Bar** will continue to operate on the lower level. It serves the best seafood in town. It sometimes has as many as 12 different kinds of oysters. Open Monday through Friday from 11:30 a.m. to 9:30 p.m. Closed Saturday and Sunday. Now is the time to enjoy a pre-theatre clam chowder, oysters or any one of a number of excellent seafood specialties. After the theatre, you will be having a light supper.

Evening

Stroll West on 44th St., across Fifth Ave. As you continue, you will pass the **New York Yacht Club** at 37 W. 44th St. Stop in ⑭ front or cross the street to get a better perspective on this Beaux Arts facade which represents the sterns of ships overhanging the sidewalk. Decorations in the three window bays include ropes, anchors, ocean waves and dolphins. Walk past the Algonquin Hotel, where you will dine later tonight.

Continue west for one more block, past the old Belasco Theatre and a lot of rundown buildings. Suddenly you are on Broadway, with **Times Square** to your left and Duffy Square to your right. You saw this space during the day, now you are seeing it in the evening, with the lights glowing; it has a completely different feel at night. Take a few minutes to enjoy the center of this famous neon world.

(17) (18) Cross Broadway, continue west on 44th St. On your left is the famous **Sardi's Restaurant** and on your right is **Schubert Alley**, a promenade for theatergoers. Chances are your theater is within stone-throwing distance of this place.

(16) (15) After the theater, walk through **Times Square** again to enjoy the energy, lights and excitement of this place. For your third and last evening on this tour, I recommend one of the most special New York urban spaces I know, the lobby of the **Algonquin Hotel**, for a late supper.

Walk east on 44th St. The hotel is located between Fifth and Sixth Aves. This was the home of the famous literary Round Table in the 1920's; the place where humorists Dorothy Parker and Robert Benchley hung out with Harold Ross, founding editor of the New Yorker. Today, the original table sits unmarked in the Oak Room just like all the other round tables. In its glory days it sat in the Rose Room where the semicircular bar is located. A television documentary called this phenomenon, *The Ten-Year Lunch*, which began in 1919 and ended with the Wall Street crash and the Depression. In the spring of 1987 the hotel changed hands; it is now owned by Caesar Park Hotels, a subsidiary of Aoki Corporation of Tokyo. They have promised not to make major changes. Fortunately the hotel was recently given landmark status by the city's Landmarks Preservation Commission. Heaven knows what Dorothy Parker would have dreamed up to say about this state of affairs.

Your reservation will net you a tiny table in the lobby, surrounded by the number of easy chairs or sofas necessary for your party. The table boasts a funny little bell to call the waiter. Just hit it once; it is considered gauche to be insistent. Then just relax and look around. I almost always see some famous person I recognize or think I should recognize. I do have to admit that until my daughter and her family moved to New York, this was my hotel, partly because I loved going down in the elevator in the morning with Peter Ustinov or E. G. Marshall. It is also the only hotel I ever stayed at that kept "my" hotel card, and greeted me by saying, "We're so glad to see you again."

Inspect the buffet table to decide whether you want their wonderful chicken salad, fruit compote or a slice of one of their remarkable cakes. It is all good. Expensive, but good.

Enjoy this old room with the grandfather clock, worn upholstery covering old pieces of furniture, and starched napkins. In addition to all the new vest-pocket parks, sparkling atriums, and promenades, this, too, is an extraordinary New York space.

During the past three days you have entered some of the very public and some of the private glories of the city. You have a new idea how people survive in this concrete jungle. You now know that while there is a lot of concrete, there are life-enhancing green spaces and humane touches in this big city. You have found some of the real treasure troves of The Big Apple.

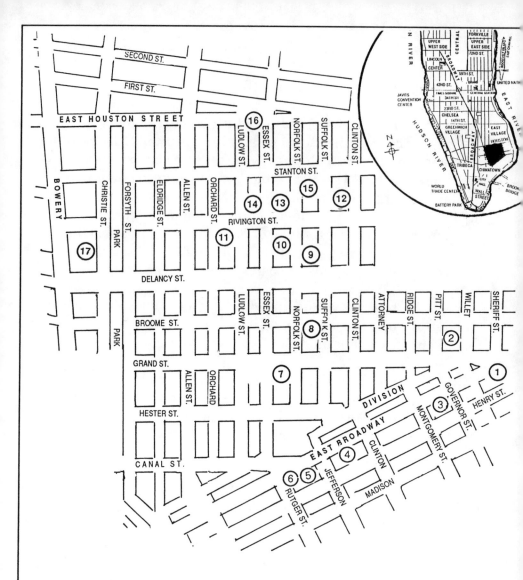

Jewish **Day 1**

1. East Side Mikvah
2. Bialystoker Synagogue
3. Henry St. Settlement House
4. Educational Alliance
5. Forward Building
6. Location of old Garden Cafeteria
7. Kossar's Bakery
8. Beth Hamedrash Hagodol Synagogue
9. Ratner's Restaurant
10. Essex Market
11. First Romanian-American Congregation
12. Streit's Matzoth Factory
13. Schapiro's Wine Co.
14. Economy Candy
15. Congregation Anseh Slonim
16. Katz's Deli
17. Sammy's Roumanian Jewish Restaurant

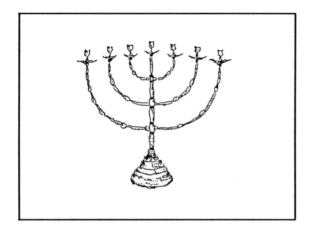

Jewish New York

Jacob Barsimon, a refugee from Brazil, is reputed to be the first Jewish person to set foot in North America. The year was 1654. Earlier that year, after 24 years of Dutch rule, Brazil had been overrun by the Portuguese who encouraged Jews to emigrate.

Within a month of Barsimon's arrival, five Jewish families, including 23 men, women and children, landed in New Amsterdam. These Sephardic Jews, descendants of Spanish and Portuguese Jews from the Iberian peninsula, were headed to Holland to escape religious persecution in Portuguese Brazil. Pirates overtook their ship, which in turn was captured by a French ship. The captain charged them for a trip to Amsterdam, but brought them to New Amsterdam instead. Peter Stuyvesant, governor of the colony, attempted to prevent their landing, but the Dutch West Indies Company, which included many Jewish stockholders, insisted the newcomers be permitted to land.

The first synagogue in New York City was in a rented room on Beaver St., later on the second floor of a flour mill on Mill St., in what is now the city's financial district. In 1730 the first synagogue building was built on South William St. For 100 years it was the only synagogue in the city serving the small Jewish congregation.

In the mid 1800s, Jewish immigrants from Poland, Bavaria, Germany, Austria and Hungary fled to the United States. In 1880 there were about 85,000 Jews in New York.

It was in 1881 that pogroms in Russia started a wave of Jewish emigration. By 1910 more than a million Jews were in New York; more than half of them living in the 20 blocks you will visit today.

Here, instead of the Goldina Medina, or golden streets, the refugees sought were terrible tenements and sweat shops, poverty and tuberculosis. Jews were forced into the 'needle trades' and peddling, since they were prohibited by law from most other occupations. The miserable wages, crowding, physical and mental illness and crime were relieved by the religious and intellectual life fostered by the early settlement houses, libraries, newspapers and other educational and political alliances on the Lower East Side.

The immigration law of 1924 effectively stopped new immigration and the area began to change. Today about one-third of the community is Jewish; the remainder made up of Puerto Ricans, blacks, Chinese, Italians and others. New immigrants from Asia, especially Bangladesh, are rapidly changing the Lower East Side.

Your tour today might best be described as an exercise in urban archaeology. You will see many existing places, but you must also use your imagination to reconstruct the life that once energized these streets. Much is gone, deteriorating and changing, but I love this exciting, stimulating and energetic part of New York.

Day I

Highlights: Jewish lower East side with its old synagogues, restaurants, shops, and historic landmarks.

Reservations: Dinner: Sammy's Roumanian Jewish Restaurant, 157 Chrystie St. near Delancey St. *Telephone 673-0330.* Open daily " 3 p.m. until we close."

Morning

Just a note about eating today: Though I have suggested a restaurant for your evening meal, I am not planning a specific lunch place. During your walk today, you will visit at least a dozen delis, shops and restaurants where you can eat, nibble or nosh your way around the streets. Eat when you are hungry, rest when you are tired and just enjoy the day. Believe me, there is no lack of places to fill your stomach, rest your feet or stimulate your imagination.

Start the day about 10 a.m. at the corner of East Broadway and Grand Sts. Notice the Amalgamated Cooperative apartments across the street, built in 1930, and now joined by the 1951 Hillman house development.

At 33 Grand St. is the **East Side Mikvah,** or ritularium, the last ① public ritual bath on the Lower East Side. Many synagogues had and have their own baths, but in an area where many buildings were converted into synagogues and could not afford to install their own mikvahs, these public baths were and are important. Orthodox Jewish brides take ritual baths and women use the baths monthly. Ceremonial objects, bought from non-Jews, are immersed and the baths are also used in the ceremony of conversion. Both men and women use this ritularium. Tours by appointment. Telephone 475-8514.

Or, walk across the street to the kosher dairy store. Also, stick your head in the kosher bakery next to the dairy store.

A block west to Grand St. and Bialystoker Place, is the **Bialys-** ② **toker Synagogue** (1826), built by the Methodist Episcopal Church, later bought by a Jewish congregation from Bialystok, a city and province of Russia, later Poland. The interior carvings can be seen by the light coming through pastel-colored side windows. The painted ceiling of sky and clouds is surrounded by images of goats, fish, birds, a lobster and a lion.

Note the painting of the wailing wall on the right front wall.

Walk back to East Broadway, once the center of Orthodox Judaism in New York, cross Grand Ave. and walk past Ahearn Park with the older people chatting and sunning and past the storefront synagogues, **Shteebl Row**, extending from 225 to 283 East Broadway. Most of these storefront or back-room (shteebl) synagogues are organized according to the country or town of origin. Some of these groups are Hasidic; others are ultra-Orthodox. The men still wear beards, side curls, black clothing and wide-brimmed hats.

③ One block south is Henry St., home of the **Henry Street Settlement House**, one of the nation's first social service agencies. Its founder, Lillian Wald, is revered in this community. Her battle against disease, poverty and ignorance is legendary. It continues to serve the neighborhood with day care, programs for the elderly, schools for the handicapped, opportunities for employment and credit union.

Back to East Broadway. As you cross Montgomery St., notice the ornate apartment building on your left and the far away sight of the World Trade Center's twin towers looming on the horizon.

You will pass the **Young Israel Synagogue** (229 East Broadway), formed for a group of second-generation Orthodox Jews who promote Orthodox living, but have accepted American styles and culture.

By the time you reach Clinton St., you will begin to notice the influx of the Chinese. At 197 East Broadway, you will pass the ④ **Educational Alliance**, once the Hebrew Institute, the intellectual heart of the Jewish ghetto. The Alliance held classes in English and civics for immigrant children and adults, operated a library, ran social programs and provided cultural classes and theater. Today it still aids the aged and poor, providing health services, a day care center and programs for alcoholics, runaways and street youth.

The **Seward Park Library** is located at 192 East Broadway, with a huge collection of Yiddish and Hebrew books and a collection of works on Lower East Side history. It was here that Leon Trotsky studied while living in New York.

Cross Jefferson St. to the **Forward Building** (173-75 East Broadway), once the home of the most important Yiddish daily newspaper in the country and now a Chinese church. Today its offices are uptown at 45 E. 33 St.; it is the only surviving Yiddish daily. Its editor, Abraham Cahan (1860-1951), was one of the most important forces in the community, using the newspaper to highlight life on the East Side, fulminate against abuses, and offer an outlet for people to speak their minds in the most famous feature of the paper, the Bintel Brief (Bundle of Letters), the precursor to Dear Abby.

You are now at the intersection of Canal, East Broadway, and Rutgers, which becomes Essex St. on the north side of East Broadway. If you were to continue west on East Broadway, in about four or five long blocks you would come to Chatham Square, just south of Chinatown. Here you would find the oldest Jewish landmark in North America, the **First Shearith Israel** (Remnant of Israel) **Graveyard**, the second Jewish burial ground in Manhattan (the location of the first is unknown.) Eighteen Jewish solders from the Revolutionary War are buried here along with Abraham de Lucene, who brought the first Torah scroll to North America, and Gershon Mendes Seixas, the first American-born rabbi, friend of George Washington.

If you walk down to see the cemetery, retrace your steps on East Broadway to Number 165 (between Rutgers and Jefferson Sts.) to what was once the **Garden Cafeteria**, a restaurant with a long history of serving Jewish labor leaders, actors and newspaper reporters.

One day, I had looked forward to a late morning break with coffee and a bagel in company with my memories of the men and women who spent so many hours here. As I walked past the windows, there were smoked ducks hanging in a row. The Garden Cafeteria is now the Wing Shoon Restaurant. The bagels and blintzes are gone and so is the mural of early days. Times change.

Cross the intersection, walk north on Essex St., **the heart of the Jewish center.** At 13 Essex is Zelig Blumenthal's store selling ritual articles, and **Weinfeld's** is at number 19, with a huge assortment of Yarmulkes.

At one time, three pickle shops greeted you at #35 Essex by sight and smell: **Pickleman's, Hollander Kosher Pickle Stop** and **Guss's Pickle Stand.** Pickleman's is no more and Hollander and Guss have joined forces in one store. The pickle barrels still stand on the sidewalk yielding their unforgettable odors of spices, horseradish and dill and you can still buy the sours, half-sours and hot peppers.

Leibel Bistritzky's kosher grocery store used to be at 27 1/2 Essex; it has moved down the street to Number 39. Every day at 4 p.m. a minyan, a Jewish prayer service requiring ten men, is still held behind its closed doors.

At Number 45 Essex, climb the cast iron stairway to visit a store of antique (18th and 19th-century) Jewish art. Turn left on Grand to visit Number 345, **Grand Sterling**, with its reproductions of silver ceremonial objects and other silver pieces. This may be the finest store of its kind anywhere.

(7) To your right on Grand, off Essex, is the famous **Kossar's** at Number 367 Grand. Here you can buy the fragrant bialys, wonderful warm chewy onion rolls, for 30 cents apiece. Walk one more block north on Essex to Broome St., turn right one block to Norfolk. A few steps to your right at Number 60 Nor-

(8) folk you will see **Beth Hamedrash Hagodol Synagogue**, the first Russian-Jewish Orthodox synagogue in the country. The pale blue ceiling looks down on the leather-covered seats. Note the Chinese Hong Ning housing for the elderly next door to the synagogue.

(9) North on Norfolk to Delancy St. and on your right is **Ratner's** at Number 138 Delancey, the most famous of all New York's

dairy restaurants, burned down in 1990, and now reopened.

One block west to Essex, turn right to the block-long **Essex** ⑩
Street Market with vegetable, fruit and fish stands. Here you
will find Santeria magic books next to Dristan and plaster
saints, clothing and jewelry next to bananas and a one-chair
barber shop. The smells are overpowering.

Continue north on Essex to Rivington St., turn left a block and
a half to see the **First Roumanian Shul** (1885), a well cared for ⑪
synagogue, famous for its cantors, including the most famous
of all, Yossel Rosenblatt. Women sit in a side room, next to the
very small meeting room. Back to Essex St. On the other side of
Essex, at Number 150 Rivington is **Streit's Matzoth Company,** ⑫
the only Manhattan bakery still producing matzoth (un-
leavened bread). You can watch the bakers at work on the un-
believably ancient machines and conveyor belts. If you look
interested and friendly, they may break off a piece of the warm
bread for you.

As you walk west on Rivington, look overhead to see the
laundry framing the fire escapes. At 126 Rivington visit
Schapiro's, the oldest kosher winery in America (1899). The ⑬
sign reads, "The Wine you Can Almost Cut With a Knife." On
Sundays from 11 a.m. to 5 p.m. you can tour the cellars and
sample the wines in the tasting room. In fact, almost any day
you stop in, they will offer you a sample of their wine.

Back to the corner of Essex and Rivington. A few steps to 108
Rivington and **Economy Candy** with its huge tubs of halvah, ⑭
home-made and hand-dipped chocolates and marzipan.

At 147 Essex you can find Jewish books, tapes and records at
Louis Stavsky. You can also find good conversation at
Stavsky's.

At the corner of Essex and Stanton Sts., turn right one block to
Norfolk St. and right again. At Number 172 Norfolk is **Con-** ⑮
gregation Anshe Slonim, the oldest, barely surviving,
synagogue in the city, built in 1850.

As I was facing the sad old synagogue, I heard the sound of children's voices behind me. As I turned, I realized there was a school and a playground across the street. Later I visited with one of the teachers who told me how the neighborhood was changing as the result of new immigrants, many from Asia, especially Bangladesh. She talked about how the parents are so eager for their children to learn English and to do well in school. The echoes of the early Jewish immigrants rang in my ears. It is sad to see the old change and pass away, but it is exciting to feel the vitality from the newest citizens.

Noon

Walk north on Norfolk to Houston St., turn left and walk one block to the biggest deli on the Lower East Side, (16) **Katz's**. I have to admit it is also my favorite.

On my first visit to this part of New York, my cabbie invited me to Katz's for lunch. I am not sure I would have had the nerve to brave the huge men behind the counters with their long, sharp knives and loud voices as they demand your order. But my friend guided me through my first Lower East Side self-service cafeteria: huge pastrami sandwich, greasy French fries, enormous garlic pickles and cream soda. Tables in the center of the huge room are for the self-servers; tables against the walls are for waiter-service. If you make a mistake, the waiters will tell you in loud voices.

Be sure you remember to take a ticket from the woman seated near the door. Each time you order something at the counter, they demand your ticket to mark the cost of each item you order. My first meal of a three-inch pastrami sandwich, two pickles, a humongous plate of French fries and a Dr. Brown's cream soda cost me $6.75. It is a bit pricier today.

Afternoon

Walk west two blocks on Houston to **Orchard St**. This street of shops was once filled with pushcarts and peddlers. Sunday is the best day for crowds, noise and fun on Orchard

Street; it is even closed to traffic on Sundays. Hang on to your wallet and only let go of your money after serious bargaining. It is expected.

Return to Houston on Orchard St., turn left, and you will come to **Moishe's Bakery** at Number 181 with bialys, bagels, black bread, corn rye and wonderful desserts: mandelbrot, Russian babkas and coffee cakes. Adjacent is **Ben's Cheese Shop** with all its fruit flavored cheeses and farm butter. New wooden fronts have improved the look of the exteriors of these two shops, but, fortunately, the insides have remained the same.

Then comes **Russ and Daughters** for smoked fish, candied fruit and other gourmet items and two blocks further at Number 137 Houston is **Yonah Schimmel's Knishes Bakery**. It almost looks too run-down to enter, but don't let that stop you. It is *The* knish shop. (A knish is a thin pastry crust wrapped around a variety of fillings.) All of these places are inexpensive.

Evening

By now it should be late afternoon; if it isn't, you have not been paying attention. If you have not eaten at every restaurant, cafe or shop you passed, you may be ready for dinner. Walk one block from the knish bakery to Chrystie St., turn left and south about two blocks to 157 Chrystie St. near Delancey St. and **Sammy's Roumanian Jewish Restaurant**. ⑰

This is one of the liveliest and most interesting restaurants in the area. However, note that it is not kosher. Do not let the few deflated balloons and sorry crepe paper streamers deter you from enjoying this cholesterol heaven. And just ignore the walls, covered with photos and business cards. Plan to eat the richest food in town.

It opens at 3 p.m. and stays open til it closes, as they say. The portions are huge, so plan to share. Try the stuffed cabbage or grilled meats. I love the potato pancakes. I don't drink, but they tell me the red wine is awful. You will find milk, chocolate syrup and seltzer on each table; make your own egg cream.

After a long day, filled with so much walking, imagining and eating, just relax at Sammy's tonight and enjoy the music which is usually pretty good; often a violin and piano. Save the Yiddish Theatre for tomorrow.

Day 2

Highlights: The **Diamond Center, synagogues,** the **Jewish Museum** exhibitions, **Zabar's** and **Lincoln Center.**

Reservations: Tours of the **Central Synagogue** are available by appointment. *Call 838-5122.* Dinner reservations: **Levana's,** 141 W. 69th St. Telephone 877-8457. If you plan to go to the theatre, order your tickets. For information about Jewish theatre performances, call the Hebrew Actors' Union *674-1923.*

For information on Jewish concerts or other programs, check the newspapers for events scheduled by the Hebrew Arts School, the American Society for Jewish Music or the 92nd Street YMCA. There are also concerts at many of the synagogues.

Morning

Start the day at Avenue of the Americas (Sixth Ave.) and 47th Street at 10 a.m.. The first time I walked this block, I was looking for the famous **Gotham Book Mart**. I had no idea I had stumbled into the **diamond market,** the street on which 80 per- (1) cent of all diamonds coming into the country are handled. I began to know something unusual was happening when I realized I was surrounded by Hasidic Jews, distinguishable by their beards, sidelocks, large black hats and long coats.

Later, I learned that this was the center of the **diamond retail and wholesale business.** Jews have been diamond dealers for centuries in Europe. Diamonds were always a valuable and portable asset for people who were often fleeing persecution.

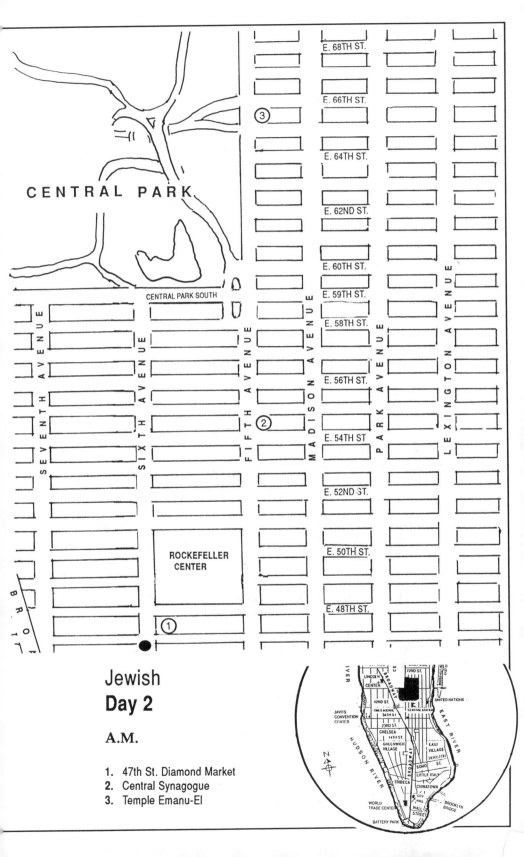

CENTRAL PARK

CENTRAL PARK SOUTH

E. 68TH ST.
E. 66TH ST.
E. 64TH ST.
E. 62ND ST.
E. 60TH ST.
E. 59TH ST.
E. 58TH ST.
E. 56TH ST.
E. 54TH ST
E. 52ND ST.
E. 50TH ST.
E. 48TH ST.

SEVENTH AVENUE
SIXTH AVENUE
FIFTH AVENUE
MADISON AVENUE
PARK AVENUE
LEXINGTON AVENUE

BROADWAY

ROCKEFELLER
CENTER

Jewish
Day 2

A.M.

1. 47th St. Diamond Market
2. Central Synagogue
3. Temple Emanu-El

The flexibility of working hours attracted Orthodox Jews, who were able to take time off for afternoon prayers and get home before the Sabbath, and the trade of stone-cutting was one of the few open to Jews.

The street level is filled with jewelry shops and little restaurants, plus the Gotham Book Mart. The real business for the diamond dealers is transacted in upstairs offices and shops. If you are interested in buying, come equipped with some knowledge of retail prices and be prepared to bargain.

If you want to just watch, walk to 4 W 47th St. and the **Diamond Dairy** in the Jeweler's National Exchange. This kosher restaurant is in a glassed-in gallery above the exchange, a covered arcade of jewelry stalls. Walk to the back of the exchange to the steep stairway which will take you to the restaurant. You can watch and listen and eat your blintzes, all at the same time.

As you leave the exchange, you are just a few steps from Fifth Ave. Walk north on Fifth to 55th St., then three blocks east to Lexington and the Central Synagogue. The walk along Fifth Ave. is one of the richest and most interesting in town.

② The **Central Synagogue** (1872) is the oldest one in continual use in the state and was designed by the first Jew to practice architecture in New York, Henry Fernbach. This building is one of the finest examples of Moorish Revival architecture in New York. Notice the onion-shaped copper domes, the interior stencilling and the brownstone facade.

③ Walk north on Lexington to 65th St., turn left to Fifth Ave. and **Temple Emanu-El**, the largest Reform temple in the world. Founded by German Reform Jews, this church seats 2,500 people, more than St. Patrick's Cathedral. Notice the Tiffany stained glass windows above the ark. Tours are conducted often during the day. It is open Sunday through Thursday from 10 a.m. to 5 p.m., and Saturday from noon to 5 p.m.

The House of Living Judaism, headquarters of the Reform

movement in the United States and many other groups, is located at 838 Fifth Avenue, next to Temple Emanu-el. Judaic exhibits are on display on the ground floor.

Jump into a cab to go to the renovated **Jewish Museum**, located at the corner of Fifth Ave. and 92nd St. It is open Sunday, Monday, Wednesday and Thursday from 11 a.m. to 5:45 p.m.; Tuesday from 11 a.m. to 8 p.m. It is closed on Friday, Saturday and major legal and Jewish holidays. Admission.

After two years of renovation and expansion, the museum reopened in 1993 in what was once the Warburg mansion. You may see the museum's extensive permanent collections as well as whatever its temporary exhibitions may be. In addition, check the schedule for films and lectures. Be certain to visit the fascinating museum shop and stop downstairs for lunch, coffee or tea at the Cafe Weissman.

Afternoon

Take a cab across Central Park to the corner of Broadway and 80th St. Here you will find **Zabar's**, the world's most amazing food store. What began as a small Jewish deli has grown to be the eighth wonder of the food world. ①

Across the street is **H & H Bagels West**, where you may want to stop first to buy one of their fresh hot bagels.

They make about 60,000 a day, shipping all over the world. Also visit their kosher and non-kosher market. Your hot bagel may take the edge off your appetite as you walk cross the street to dive into the maelstrom of Zabar's. The store is filled with cookware, food and celebrities and the prices are excellent. Wander around until you want to sit down and have a bite to eat at their cafe, **Les Delices**. Try the cappuccino and be sure to order a dessert.

Walk south one block to 79th, turn right toward Central Park West.

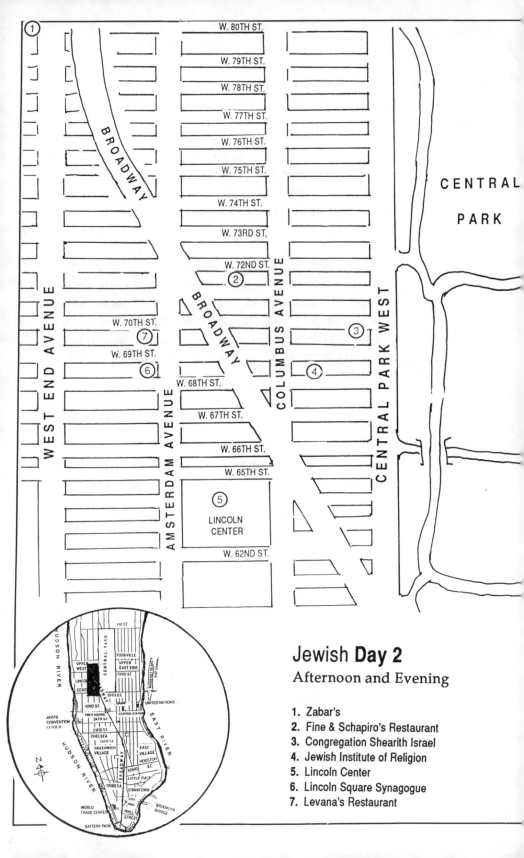

Jewish Day 2

Afternoon and Evening

1. Zabar's
2. Fine & Schapiro's Restaurant
3. Congregation Shearith Israel
4. Jewish Institute of Religion
5. Lincoln Center
6. Lincoln Square Synagogue
7. Levana's Restaurant

Walk south on Central Park West. You will be walking along the edge of the Central Park West/76th Street Historic District. At the corner of Central Park West and 72nd, you will walk past the historic **Dakota** apartments. If you choose to turn right to walk a block and a half west on 72nd W., you will come to **Fine** ② **and Shapiro's Delicatessen Restaurant,** in business since 1927. This kosher delicatessen is open daily 8:30 a.m. to 10 p.m. Everything is made in the restaurant, including the gefilte fish.

Continue south on Central Park W. to 70th St. Here you will find **Congregation Shearith Israel,** the nation's oldest Jewish ③ congregation, dating from 1654, when the first Jewish refugees from Brazil landed in the New World. Some artifacts from their first synagogue in Lower Manhattan are preserved in the "Little Synagogue" here, open during Friday and Saturday morning services.

Walk south on Central Park West, turn right on W. 68th St., to Number 40 and the **Jewish Institute of Religion**, a rabbinical ④ training school. Two blocks south is **Lincoln Center**. It is a ⑤ short walk to look at the two great Marc Chagall murals you can see through the 10-story glass facade of the Metropolitan Opera House. Just one more reminder of the many treasures in this city produced by Jewish artists.

Walk through the Center to your right to 65th St., turn left for about half a block to Amsterdam Ave., turn right four blocks to 69th and Amsterdam. Here is the **Lincoln Square Synagogue,** ⑥ its travertine exterior looking very much like Lincoln Center. This is one of the city's most popular synagogues.

Dinner

Walk to 141 W. 69th to **Levana's,** a glatt kosher restaurant. ⑦ Reservations are usually necessary. They serve a prix fixe dinner at a moderate price. The meat and fish dishes are excellent and the desserts are wonderful. It is open 5 to 11 p.m., Monday through Thursday, and 3 to 11 p.m. Sunday.

This evening, attend the Yiddish theater or Jewish musical performance you called about earlier today.

During these two days you will have explored a small part of the world's largest Jewish community, New York City. But you have only explored in Manhattan. More adventures in the Hasidic communities of Borough Park and Williamsburg in Brooklyn and other Jewish centers are still waiting for you. I limited the tours in this book to Manhattan, but there is no limiting the adventures waiting for you in other sections of this remarkable city.

Additional information

A very special new museum is currently under construction in lower Manhattan's Battery Park City. **A Living Memorial to the Holocaust-Museum of Jewish Heritage** is being built on a stunning waterfront site directly opposite the Statue of Liberty and Ellis Island. The museum is scheduled to open during the latter half of 1997.

The museum's core exhibition will be organized around three themes:

Early 20th Century Jewish Life: The first chapter of the museum's narrative will describe the dynamic and vibrant Jewish communities that thrived throughout the world.

War against the Jews: The second chapter will explore the unimaginable devastation of the Holocaust, as recorded and recalled manly by Jews before they perished as well as by those who managed to survive Jewish Renewal.

The third chapter will examine the renewal of Jewish life during the past half century, principally in Israel and the United States.

The 30,000-square-foot facility was designed by the architectural firm of Kevin Roche, John Dinkeloo and Associates. With its strikingly symbolic six sides and distinctive steeped louvred roof rising 85 feet in the air, the building is destined to become a New York City landmark.

The museum will be one of only five institutions around the world designated as a repository for video testimonies gathered by Steven Spielberg's Survivors of the Shoah Visual History Foundation, the world's largest collection of its kind.

In advance of the public opening, the museum is operating a series of public education and outreach programs, including an annual film and discussion series, a speaker's bureau and several special and traveling exhibitions. The museum also publishes a quarterly newsletter.

For additional information about plans for the museum and programs, call *212-687-9141*.

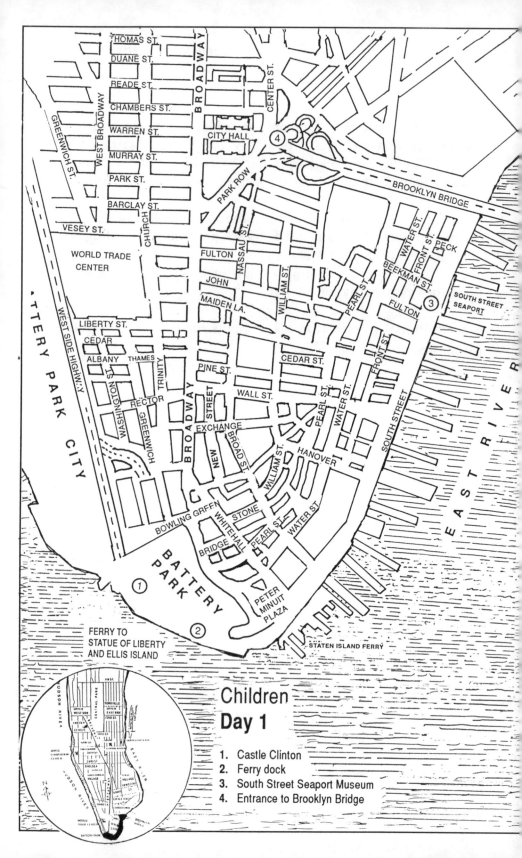

Children
Day 1

1. Castle Clinton
2. Ferry dock
3. South Street Seaport Museum
4. Entrance to Brooklyn Bridge

Children's New York

New York can become even more extraordinary when seen through the eyes of a child. Those of you who are fortunate enough to accompany a young person through the city will see its sights and enchantments with a new vision.

I have a grandson who lives in Manhattan, and I love walking around the city with him. Several of these tours were tested on John. These plans are aimed at children between the ages of six and thirteen and their parents of any age.

Day 1

Highlights: Statue of Liberty and **American Museum of Immigration, Ellis Island, South Street Seaport, Brooklyn Bridge,** and a **sailboat ride.**

Reservations: Pioneer Schooner. South Street Seaport. *Telephone 669-9416.* Reservations accepted, but not necessary.

Morning

Start your day at **Battery Park,** where the Circle Line operates sailings to the **Statue of Liberty** and the **American**

Museum of Immigration and Ellis Island. The ferries leave from the South Ferry, every hour on the hour, from 9 a.m. to 4 p.m. There are additional sailings Saturday, Sunday and holidays from April through October. Sailings are every half-hour during July and August starting at 10:30 a.m.

① Cab to the Battery in time for the 9 a.m. sailing. Get your tickets at **Castle Clinton**. Round trip fares include both the Statue of Liberty and Ellis Islands and cost $7 for adults; $3 for children, 11 years and under. No reservations are necessary. There are refreshment and souvenir counters on board, but prices are higher than on shore. The round trip takes about 45 minutes. A visit, including climbing the statue and a tour to the museums, will take about three hours. Refreshments are available on the island, but picnicking is not encouraged. Because these are such popular attractions, I suggest going early in the morning; later on, it is often very crowded.

The renovated **Statue of Liberty** reopened in the summer of 1986. More than $200 million was raised to strengthen and beautify the 152-foot-tall Lady Liberty, which weighs 18,000 pounds, has a 35-foot waist and a four-and-a-half-foot nose. The renovated Ellis Island opened in 1990.

② Walk to the **Ferry Dock**. When you board the ferry, walk up the steps to the top deck where you can enjoy the views of the skyline of Manhattan and the statue. Everybody rushes to get off the boat; relax and wait for the crowd to ease.

Follow the path around to your right toward the base of the statue. I recommend walking up to the **third level**, an easy walk, and then out onto the promenade. There are always long lines for the elevator to the base of the pedestal. Frankly, I think the lines are too long for children and the angle for viewing the lady is not good. And the long walk up the stairs to the crown is not worth either the time or energy, particularly with children. I think you can get a better view of the statue from the promenade on the third floor and an equally fine view of Manhattan, all without exhaustion or expenditure of hours of your time.

Before you walk to the third level, notice the original torch exhibited on the main floor. It will give all of you a sense of the size of the statue.

The **Immigration Exhibition** is on the third floor. I think your children will love the photographs of immigrants, who could be their ancestors, arriving in America. Many of the displays have audio presentations which are fun for the children to use.

The **Statue of Liberty exhibition** is on the second level with equally fascinating memorabilia and presentations. Note: Bathrooms are on the balcony level.

Wander around to the front of the island, facing Manhattan, and let the children enjoy the open space and the great views. This extraordinary island takes time to enjoy. If you hurry, you will miss much of its charm.

Take the **ferry,** included in the price of your round-trip ticket, to **Ellis Island**. Visit the sea wall, with its copper panels bearing names of families that passed through Ellis Island, and enjoy another great view of New York.

Inside the building, depending on the ages of your children, decide whether to view the **30-minute film** about the island.

Visit the huge baggage room and upstairs' **Registry Room** and particularly the room with **Treasures from Home,** so your children can see some of the things immigrants actually carried from overseas to their new home here in America.

If you are hungry, there is a restaurant here which serves a variety of ethnic foods and in nice weather has a lovely terrace.

Otherwise, wait till you return to Manhattan.

Noon

Walk back toward the dock, and the short ferry ride to Manhattan. In the interest of saving your energy and your

children's feet, I suggest taking a cab the 10 or 12 blocks to the
③ **South Street Seaport Museum** at Fulton St. and the East River.

There are dozens of places to eat in the great Pier 17, which
sticks out into the East River. An escalator will take you to the
third floor and the fast food counters.

Afternoon

At **Fulton St.**, once the site of the famous fish market and
home to the great river traffic of the 19th-century, is a new
and restored landmark district, including pedestrian
walkways, waterfront piers with historic ships to visit, shops,
restaurants, street performers and special events. Every week
there are new diversions added.

Believe me, your children will love this place. A ticket booth
and information center is located in the middle of the docks.
Visit the piers and climb aboard the ships: the four-masted
Peking, the fishing schooner *Lettie G. Howard* and the full-
rigged *Wavertree*. The steam ferry, *Major General Wm. H. Hart*,
serves as the seaport waterfront office. Some of the ships may
be undergoing restoration and will not be boardable, but there
will always be a number of them ready for visitors.

Around the corner at 165 John St. is the **Children's Center**,
where your youngsters can climb a ship's rigging, try on
sailor's clothes, lie in a bunk or secure sails. Every Saturday the
center conducts special workshops to learn a sea chantey, make
a whale hat, create a mural of the underwater world or other
projects.

The great new glass pavilion which extends toward the East
River is filled with wonderful shops, restaurants and
promenades.

The 40-passenger sailing schooner, *Pioneer*, sails from May to
the middle of September. Call 748-8786 to make reservations
and check on sailing times and schedules. Since both change
regularly, this is better advice than any I could give you at this

writing. Reservations are heavily encouraged.

There is no food available on the boat, so if you think your youngsters will be hungry, bring some food and drinks with you. Take-away food is available at many of the restaurants at the seaport.

If by any chance you still have energy to burn, take a cab to the entrance to the walkway on **Brooklyn Bridge**, in front of City ④ Hall. I suspect this is the most beautiful structure in New York. It was the world's first steel suspension bridge.

An elevated pedestrian promenade takes you above the traffic and across to Brooklyn. Walk to the center of the bridge, over the East River, for one of the most beautiful views in town. Take hold of the steel cables to feel the bridge's pulse. It is alive. The view is particularly lovely as the lights go on in the city.

Walk back to City Hall, grab a cab and go back to your hotel or wherever you are staying. You might want to enjoy the luxury of room service for supper tonight. It is time for the parents to rest.

Day 2

Highlights: Empire State Building, United Nations, Radio City Music Hall, AT&T Infoquest Center and a deli.

Reservations: Radio City Music Hall tickets. 50th St. and Sixth Ave. Charge tickets by phone. *Telephone: 247-4777.* Most credit cards are accepted. For other music hall information, Telephone 632-4000.

Morning

Cab to the **Empire State Building,** on Fifth Ave. between ① 33rd and 34th Sts. about 9:30 a.m. This is not the world's tallest building any longer, but it is still a magical skyscraper.

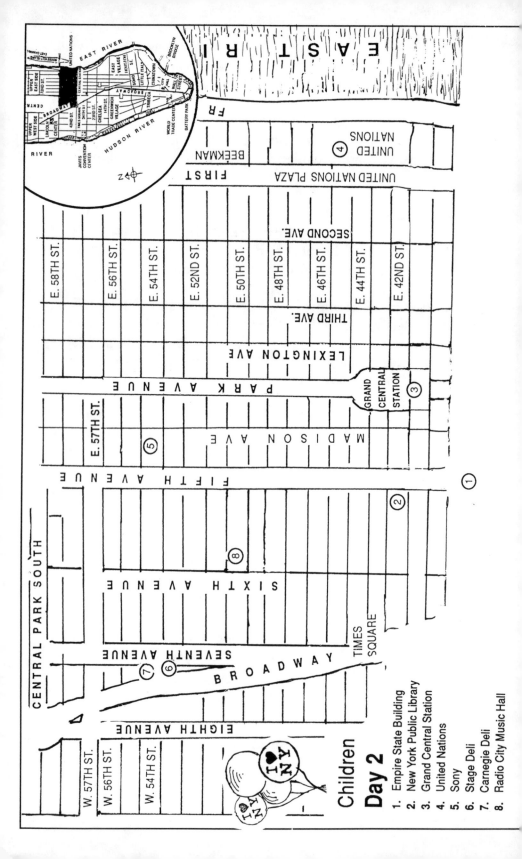

Children
Day 2

1. Empire State Building
2. New York Public Library
3. Grand Central Station
4. United Nations
5. Sony
6. Stage Deli
7. Carnegie Deli
8. Radio City Music Hall

Note the illuminated panels in the marble-lined lobby showing the eight wonders of the world, the traditional seven plus the Empire State Building.

The ticket office for the observation deck is located on the Concourse, one level below the Main Lobby, and is reached by escalators. Tickets may be used any time and are not limited to day of purchase. Be sure to pick up a brochure which will help you identify sights from the Observatory, which is open seven days a week from 9 a.m. to 11:30 p.m. An outdoor promenade, food, drink, souvenir counters and inside viewing are located on the 86th floor, which is reached by high speed automatic elevators; the 102nd floor Observatory is enclosed. Admission. The views are spectacular. *On a Clear Day You Can See Forever* must have been written with this place in mind. Ships can be seen 40 miles at sea; visibility on a clear day is 80 miles.

Before you leave, you and your children may want to try the New York Skyride, virtual New York. This is an exciting way to see the city on film, but with all the thrills of flight simulation. Fasten your seat belts, pay the costs of $9 for adults and $7 for kids and seniors — and take off.

You are now headed for the **United Nations.** You can either walk the thirteen blocks or take a cab. If your children are small, you may want to cab. If you decide to see the sights on the way, walk north on Fifth Ave., past **Lord and Taylor** department store. Between 40th and 42nd Sts., you will pass the main branch of the **New York Public Library**. Notice the wonderful ② marble lions, named Patience and Fortitude.

Turn right on 42nd St. Between Madison and Park Avs. is the **Lincoln Building**; in the lobby is a small version of the seated Lincoln, a copy of the Lincoln Memorial in Washington, D.C. Next you pass **Grand Central Station** on your left. It is worth a ③ look. I like the entrance off Vanderbilt Ave. The cavernous and somewhat commercialized interior still bears remnants of its glorious past. Look overhead to see the current renovation.

Continue east on 42nd St., past the wonderful **Bowery Savings**

Bank and the **Chrysler Building**. Take a minute to walk into the lobby of the Chrysler to see the African marble walls and inlaid wood on the elevator doors.

Continue east on 42nd to First Ave. and the lobby of the **Ford Foundation** with its extraordinary garden and a pond filled with pennies tossed by both big and little children with wishes to return to New York.

④ At this point you will have arrived at the river and the **United Nations buildings**. I will not give you a history of the UN since you will be taking a tour. Going in at the visitor's entrance on First Ave. (also called United Nations Plaza) at 45th St., you enter an international zone as you pass the 185 flags of the member nations which edge First Ave.

You pass through very tight security as you enter the building. Note the chapel on your right as you leave the secured area. The twelve-foot-high-stained glass panel is by the French artist, Marc Chagall. The chapel is a memorial to Dag Hammarskjold, former Secretary-General of the United Nations, and fifteen staff members and crew who died in a 1961 plane crash in Northern Rhodesia.

Note the replica of Russia's Sputnik, the first orbiting satellite, shot into space in 1957. This gift from the U.S.S.R. hangs overhead as you enter. At one end of the lobby is a mural, *Brotherhood*, a gift from Mexico. A moon rock, from man's first landing on the moon in Apollo 14 in 1971, is in a glass case.

Noon

You can get free tickets to buy lunch in the **Delegates Dining Room** by asking for them at the Information Desk. This is an interesting though expensive place for people watching. A coffee shop with limited seating is open daily on the public concourse from 9:30 a.m. to 5 p.m. No picnicking or box lunches.

Be sure to visit the international post office, which sells beautifully designed stamps and stationery, only obtainable at the UN. Other cards and gifts from all over the world are available in the shop.

Afternoon

Buy your tickets for the one-hour tour of the buildings, which will take you to the General Assembly Hall, where delegates and world leaders meet, and to the Security Council Chamber, where differences among nations are arbitrated. The tours leave every 15 minutes from 9:30 a.m. to 4:45 p.m. Admission. For information, telephone 913-7539.

You can receive free tickets, first-come, first-served, to attend meetings of the General Assembly and Councils, when they are in session. Tickets when available are on the main floor. Sessions are at 10:30 a.m. and 3:30 p.m.

Mid-afternoon

Grab a cab for the short trip to Madison Ave. and 56th St. to visit the **Sony Wonder** space. It is open Tuesday and ⑤ Friday from 10 a.m. to 6 p.m., Wednesday, Thursday, Saturday from 10 a.m. to 6 p.m., Sunday from noon to 6 p.m., closed Monday.

Stop at the service desk in the main lobby to get information about the center and its audio tours and headphones. Pick up your personalized Sony Wonder Card to use during your visit. Visit the history of communications bridge, the technology workshop with hands-on activities, the high definition interactive theater and all the other fascinating studios and galleries. This is a hands-on space, which I think you and your children will enjoy.

Evening

Walk three blocks west on 55th St. to Seventh Ave. The ⑥ **Stage Deli** is at 54th and Seventh; the **Carnegie Deli** at ⑦ 55th and Seventh.

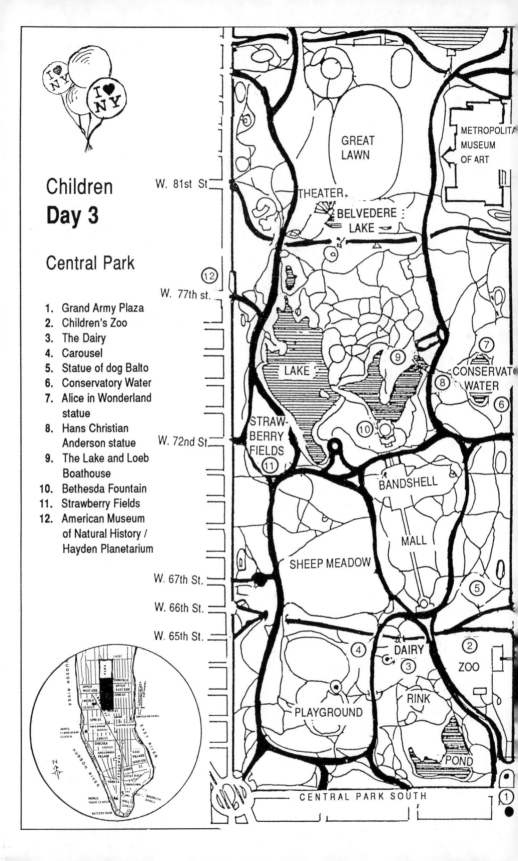

Children
Day 3

Central Park

1. Grand Army Plaza
2. Children's Zoo
3. The Dairy
4. Carousel
5. Statue of dog Balto
6. Conservatory Water
7. Alice in Wonderland statue
8. Hans Christian Anderson statue
9. The Lake and Loeb Boathouse
10. Bethesda Fountain
11. Strawberry Fields
12. American Museum of Natural History / Hayden Planetarium

W. 81st St

W. 77th st.

W. 72nd St

W. 67th St.

W. 66th St.

W. 65th St.

GREAT LAWN

METROPOLITAN MUSEUM OF ART

THEATER

BELVEDERE LAKE

LAKE

CONSERVATORY WATER

STRAWBERRY FIELDS

BANDSHELL

MALL

SHEEP MEADOW

DAIRY

ZOO

RINK

PLAYGROUND

POND

CENTRAL PARK SOUTH

If you reserved tickets for an evening show at **Radio City** ⑧ **Music Hall**, walk a block east to Sixth Ave. and five blocks south to 50th St.

Exhausted? Trek back to your hotel and relax. Tomorrow you will spend the day more leisurely in Central Park and environs.

Day 3

Highlights: Central Park, American Museum of Natural History, and the **Hayden Planetarium**.

Reservations: Boat rental at Loeb Boathouse in Central Park. *Telephone 517-2233.*

Morning

Start the day at the corner of 59th and Central Park South, ① where the horses and buggies congregate waiting for families just like yours. Take a **buggy ride**. It will be the best $34 (for one-half hour) you spend in this town and your kids will love you. If you have a particularly nice driver, and most of them are great, he may ask your child to sit up with him. Once around the park.

Ask your driver to drop you off near 65th St. and the **Central** ② **Park Zoo.** You will pass under an archway, decorated overhead by the **Delacorte Musical clock**. Bears, monkeys and other bronze animals cavort every half hour to the music of a nursery rhyme. Plan to watch this performance.

Walk south to the larger **Central Park Zoo.** Polar bears, sea lions, monkeys, and penguins all have stunning homes. There is a cafeteria and gift shop. Admission. For information telephone 861-6030.

Walk west on the 65th Transverse. The Dairy, now the park's information center, is on your left. It is a wonderful gingerbread-type house in the woods. You can find all kinds of maps and other information about the park here.

③ Just beyond the Dairy, turn left to the old-fashioned **Carousel**.
④ Listen for the music. You will all enjoy rides on this merry-go-round with wonderfully painted wooden horses.

Walk east on the 65th St. Transverse to East Drive, one of the main walks in the park. Turn left and walk north. As you arrive at the first underpass, take a detour to your right to see one of ⑤ the children's favorite statues in the park, the dog **Balto**, commemorating the lead dog of a team of huskies that carried diphtheria serum to stricken Nome, Alaska in 1925. He is rubbed shiny from the children climbing on his back.

Continue walking north on East Drive to 72nd St. On your right ⑥ is the **Conservatory Water** where children sail their model sailboats.

⑦ Two wonderful statues are located here: Alice in Wonderland with all her friends, including the Mad Hatter, welcomes ⑧ children to climb up and sit on her lap, and **Hans Christian Andersen** and his ugly duckling provide a place for storytelling in the summer.

Noon

⑨ To the west is the **Lake and Loeb Boathouse** with boats to rent and a gondola to ride. Bikes are also available. There is a snack bar and a very nice restaurant overlooking the lake. This is a wonderful place to relax for both children and parents.

Afternoon

⑩ After lunch, walk south to the 72nd St. Transverse, turn right and walk west. Look over the parapet to see the **Bethesda Fountain** and just beyond the **Cherry Hill Fountain**.

⑪ On your right you will come to **Strawberry Fields,** the section of the park memorializing the rock singer, John Lennon. It is a beautifully landscaped section of the park with a wonderful mosaic pavement emblazoned with the word *Imagine,* a tribute to Lennon's song..

Exit the park on 72nd St. and West Central Park.

Turn right and walk six blocks to the **American Museum of** ⑫ **Natural History** and the adjacent and connected **Hayden Planetarium**. In case you are hungry again, there is a cafeteria on the lower level and a nice terrace cafe where food is served outside in decent weather. Admission.

I do not know who will have the most fun here, you or your children. There are only 34 million artifacts and specimens on view, including dioramas of animal groups, dinosaurs, gems and minerals, the Star of India sapphire, and elephants.

The **Hayden Planetarium** is scheduled for a major renovation toward the end of 1996. It is difficult to tell when it may be completed. Check the New York papers and/or magazines.

Pick up a map at the information desk. Directly in front of you in **Hall 13** are dioramas of north American mammals, including the Alaska brown bear, grizzlies, wolves, mountain goats and lynxes.

Hall 10 to your left is filled with ocean life, dominated by a 94-foot model of a blue whale, obviously fake, but fun.

To your far left is **Room 5,** Man and Nature, which contains a cross-section of a giant Sequoia, 16 feet 5 inches across, cut from a tree that weighed 6,000 tons.

At the far side of the first floor is the **Hall of Minerals**. Near the entrance is a 4,700 pound slab of nephrite and opposite the door is a case containing the Star of India (563 carats) and other extraordinary gems.

Be sure to visit the **African Mammals Gallery** on the second floor. No one ever gets old enough or jaded enough to be unimpressed by the defensive circle of eight elephants located here. Just wander around to your heart's content. The dinosaur exhibitions are on the Fourth Floor.

Evening

Hungry again? The **American Museum Restaurant** in the building is open until 7:30 p.m. and boasts a children's menu. Or you can walk west on 76th St. to Broadway.

On Broadway, between 76th and 77th Sts. are two places, **The Burger Joint** and **The Pizza Joint**. They are run by the same owners and have been there for more than 20 years.

Needless to say, you can get burgers and pizzas as well as all kinds of other things children like. The adults will enjoy the food, too. Since they are jointly owned, you can order from both menus at either place.

Time for a trip back to your hotel. You have just skimmed the surface of the sights in New York begging for little visitors.

I hope this will be just the beginning of a lifelong affair with this city and its treasures.

Extra treats: If you happen to be in New York in November or December, be sure to take your children to the wonderful **Big Apple Circus**, Damrosch Park, at Lincoln Center.

This is a one-ring circus, under a new tent, with marvelous performers, both human and animal, and the seats are all in close proximity to the action. *Telephone 268-3030.*

In 1996, the **Chelsea Piers Sports and Entertainment Complex** opened. This extraordinary place is located on Piers 59 through 62, along the Hudson River from 17th to 23rd Sts. The general information number is 336-6666.

You can spend an hour, a day or a lifetime in this remarkable place. The $100 million project includes a soccer field, a gymnastics center, roller rinks, rock climbing walls, ice skating and outdoor inline-skating, a health club, golf range, basketball courts and more. There is a large swimming pool and an observation deck and the 600-seat Crab House restaurant. Other small eating places are also available, plus picnic tables and a promenade along the river. An indoor track is a quarter-mile long and the amazing heated, covered driving range permits you to purchase a $15 debit card and receive 107 balls, which are automatically delivered on the tee.

Just to give you an idea about costs: at this moment in 1996, the roller rinks charge $4 for adults, $3 for children and rent skates for $7.50 per day.

Batting cages are $1 for twelve pitches; rock climbing is $15 per class and a toddler gym is $6 per session.

Call the information number to check open times and updated costs.

Do try this amazing place.

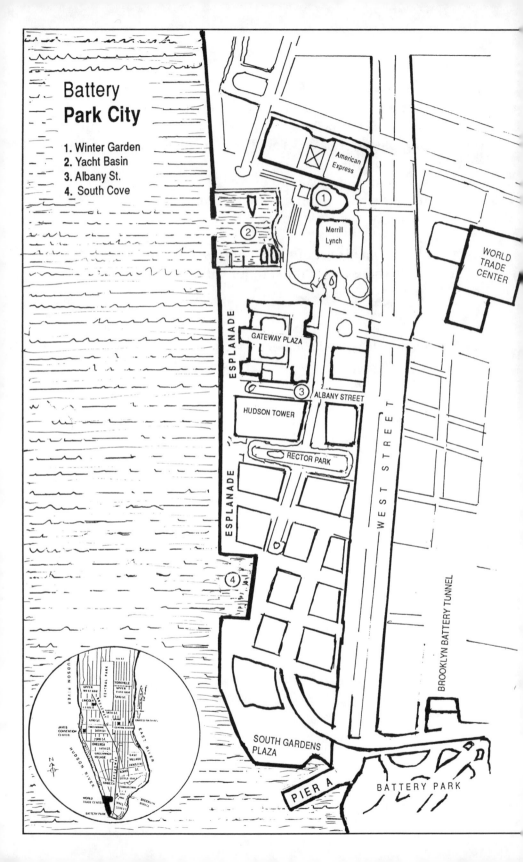

Battery Park City

1. Winter Garden
2. Yacht Basin
3. Albany St.
4. South Cove

American Express

Merrill Lynch

WORLD TRADE CENTER

ESPLANADE

GATEWAY PLAZA

ALBANY STREET

HUDSON TOWER

RECTOR PARK

ESPLANADE

WEST STREET

BROOKLYN BATTERY TUNNEL

SOUTH GARDENS PLAZA

PIER A

BATTERY PARK

Mini-walks through
Manhattan neighborhoods

New York is filled with large and small enclaves which are fascinating to explore but which did not fit into other chapters because of geography, time or scheduling. Each of the following walks can be taken during a morning or afternoon. They range in time from one-half day to a bit longer, depending on how much time the walker is willing to devote to them.

Battery Park City

Battery Park City is the newest major addition to Manhattan. Located at the southern tip of the island where the city was born, it was created as the child of the city. Its 92 acres of landfill came from the more than 24 acres of rock and earth dug up during the construction of the nearby World Trade Center.

This wonderful new section of New York was created by an extraordinary group of planners, architects and artists. It is located along the Hudson River, from Pier A, on the south, to Chamber St., on the north.

I suggest you start at the indoor Winter Garden, located between the American Express and Merrill Lynch buildings. ①

tween the **American Express** and **Merrill Lynch** buildings. This indoor public park with its 16 huge palm trees, flowing stairways and majestic public plaza is the site of many theater, dance, and art events as well as home to restaurants and shops.

You exit onto a 3 1/2-acre plaza filled with walkways, outdoor restaurants, fountains, and granite benches designed by artist Scott Burton and a wonderful fence with quotations about the city, designed by Minneapolis artist Siah Armajani. These all
(2) surround a **yacht basin**, which, if you are lucky, may be filled with boats from all over the world.

Behind you loom the towers of the **World Financial Center** and the spires of the city; in front of you are the newly created walkways along the Hudson River.

Walk south along the 1.2 mile-long **Esplanade**, with its charming street lights, benches, landscaping and public sculptures. Watch the boats as they pass by, and enjoy the sight of the **Statue of Liberty** in the distance.

(3) At **Albany St.**, you will see Ned Smyth's "The Upper Room." At the far end of the walk is the remarkable **South Cove** created
(4) by architect Stanton Eckstrut, artist Mary Miss and landscape architect, Susan Child.

Take your time to enjoy the wooden piers, wild plantings, and natural rock outcroppings as well as all the carefully designed lampposts, railings and overlooks. The park is not yet complete. Beyond South Cove, plans are underway for more gardens as well as a **Museum of Jewish Heritage**---a living memorial to the holocaust victims.

Take your time strolling through this special new area of Manhattan. It is a rewarding and uplifting experience. One of the nicest things about the Esplanade is that it has not yet been fully discovered, so it can be strangely unpopulated, although it usually is carefully patrolled by New York's finest.

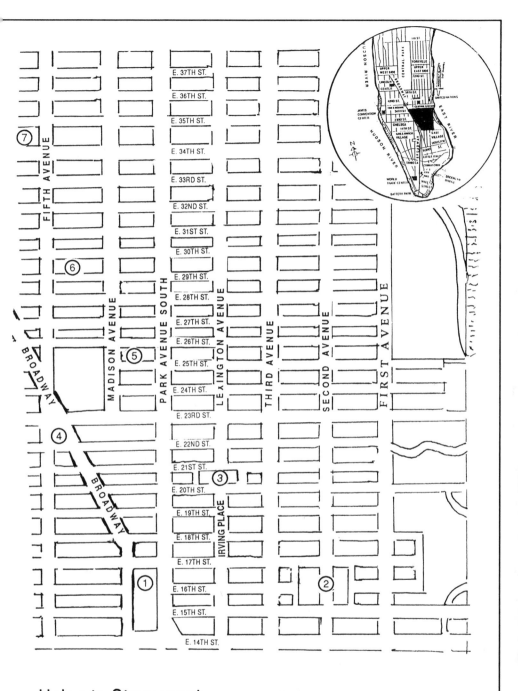

Union to Stuyvesant
to Gramercy
to Madison Squares

1. Union Square
2. Stuyvesant Square
3. Gramercy Park
4. Flatiron Building
5. Supreme Court (Appelate Division)
6. Church Around the Corner
7. Empire State Building

Union to Stuyvesant to Gramercy to Madison Squares

From square to square in one easy walk: This is an interesting and usually tourist-free part of the city. Like so many Manhattan neighborhoods, this one is unique and filled with special sights for the adventurous walker.

(1) Begin at **Union Square,** located where Park Ave. and Broadway converge, between 14th and 17th Sts. This historical center was a fancy residential area before the Civil War, a site for labor protests in the 1920s and 30s, a wretched area filled with drug dealers and other assorted ills in the 60s and 70s, and finally transformed in the 1980s by landscape artists, builders and greengrocers.

Try to visit on a Wednesday, Friday or Saturday, when the outdoor **farmer's market** is in progress. As you might expect, the produce here in the center of Manhattan is probably not inexpensive, but it is fresh and the market is filled with health foods, home-churned butter from Pennsylvania Dutch farms, homemade wines and baked goods, fresh fish and sausages and glorious plants and flowers.

Start at the south end of the square where the great equestrian statue of **George Washington** by John Quincy Adams West appears to be riding off across 14th St.. Notice the new subway kiosks. Take a minute to walk to the southwest end of the square, where you will find a statue of **Mahatma Ghandi** striding forward with his staff and sandals.

At the north end of the square is a statue of **Abraham Lincoln;** on the east is one of the **Marquis de Lafayette** by Frederic Auguste Bartholdi, and on the west a statue of a female representing charity surrounded by several children. Notice particularly the butterflies and iguanas sculpted around the base. This was originally built as a drinking fountain.

At the midpoint of the park, walk east on the crosswalk to 15th

St., continuing west about three blocks to Rutherford St; turn left. On your immediate left is the 1860 **Friends Meeting** ② **House**, a 2-story Green Revival building. The square on your right (1836) is a friendly, pleasant park, including a sculpture of **Peter Stuyvesant** by Gertrude Vanderbilt Whitney. She even included his famous pegleg.

One block further on little Rutherford St. is **St. George's Episcopal Church** (1846) and just beyond is **St. George's Chapel**. Turn left on 17th St., go two blocks to Irving Place, turn right. Across the street at **55 Irving Place** is either a place of residence for **O. Henry** or a place he often visited, depending on which researcher you read.

Continue one block to **Pete's Tavern** (1864) which claims to be the oldest continuously operating tavern in Manhattan. It is also supposed to be the place O. Henry wrote, ensconced in one of their corner booths. At any rate, it is certainly one of the pleasantest and most welcoming places in town. At noon they feature one of the best lunches at the best price in town. For about $8 you can get a cup of soup, a huge sandwich (corned beef, pastrami, ham, turkey, etc.) with potato salad and coleslaw on the side.

Across the street is another very nice restaurant, **A Friend of the Farmer's**. During the week it is not overcrowded, but on Saturday and Sunday, the lines for brunch are long. It features good, fresh, reasonably priced food. Try the sugar scones if you are not on a diet. They are spectacular.

Continue north on Irving Place about a block to **Gramercy** ③ **Park**. You are now facing the most London-like block in Manhattan. This is the only remaining private park in the city. Established in 1831, it is open only to residents in the surroundings buildings who have keys.

Plan to walk around the periphery of the park. On your left at #16 is the **Players Club**, established by the great actor **Edwin Booth**, whose statue is located in the center of the private park.

Just beyond at #15 is the **National Arts Club**. Notice the exterior medallions of Goethe, John Milton, Dante and Benjamin Franklin.

On the west side of the park is a row of Greek Revival town houses. **Number 4** was the home of Mayor James Harper (elected 1881). Note the pair of gas-lit lamps in front and the wrought iron balconies. Walk around the corner to Gramercy Park North and the hotel at the corner of Lexington Ave.

On the east side of the park is **#36**, with its concrete knights in armor and **#34** with its red turrets. The **Brotherhood Synagogue** and holocaust memorial are at the far corner. Walk east to **#129** Gramercy Park South, which is one of the most famous addresses and handsomest buildings on the square.

Continue one block to Park Ave., turn right. Walk past architect James Renwick's 1846 **Calvary Episcopal Church** with its pretty garden at 21st St. Walk two more blocks to 23rd St., turn left. Stay on the south side of the street, opposite the enormous **Metropolitan Life Insurance Co.** Look up to see the 4-sided clock, 4 feet taller than London's Big Ben.

Go west one more block to Madison Ave. Across the street on your right is Madison Square. Straight ahead is the famous ④ **Flatiron Building**. Take a minute to cross the streets to the Flatiron so you can look straight up to its roof from its prow. This triangular beauty (1902) looks just like an ocean liner about to set sail. Its cast iron prow is now the home for C. F. Company, an Italian men's sportswear store, on the ground floor. They kept the original columns and ornate ceiling plaster work and added new architectural details to the store.

Cross the street to **Madison Square** (1847). At the north end is arguably the best piece of outdoor sculpture in Manhattan: the statue of **Admiral David Farragut** by August Saint-Gaudens (1880).

Across the street on 25th St. is the Appellate Division of the ⑤ **Supreme Court of the State of New York**, an impressive name for an impressive building by Cass Gilbert (1928). Take some time to explore the exterior sculptural details, including the historical figures important in the field of law in many cultures. Statues of **Force** and **Wisdom** are on either side of the main entrance. The interior walls of the lobby are filled with a frieze called **Transmission of the Law,** unveiling the progress of the law. Ask for the informative printed brochure from the helpful guard.

But the best is saved for the courtroom itself with its magnificent stained glass dome, carvings, friezes and magnificent furniture. Court usually convenes at 2 p.m. on weekdays and you can see the courtroom then.

Walk one more block north on Madison Ave. The **New York Life Insurance Building** (1928) by Cass Gilbert is between 26th and 27th St.s. Walk into the lobby to see its painted ceilings, elevator doors and other details.

You can end your walk at this point, or if you are feeling energetic, continue a couple of blocks on Madison to 29th St., turn left to see the **Little Church Around the Corner** (Church of the ⑥ Transfiguration.) This is commonly known as the actor's church, following the refusal of a nearby church to hold an actor's funeral. They are reported to have said, "We don't accept actors here, but there's a little church around the corner that will." Strangely enough, it is said that now there are more wedding ceremonies held here than in any church in the world. It is set back from the street with lovely gardens and plantings around its buildings.

A block further west at 29th St. and 5th Ave. is Norman Vincent Peale's famous **Marble Collegiate Church**. This Dutch Reform church was established by Peter Minuit in 1628 and has been kept relatively unchanged.

And if you insist on walking further, five blocks north on Fifth ⑦ Ave. will bring you to the **Empire State Building**.

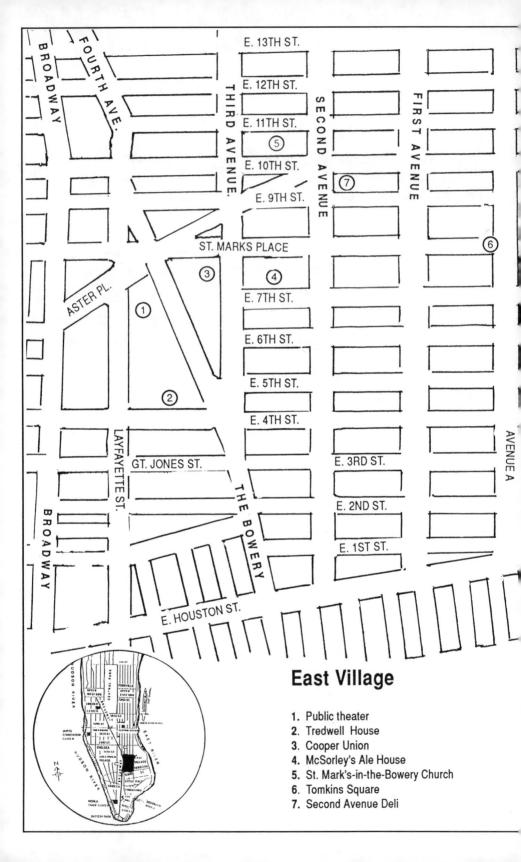

East Village

1. Public theater
2. Tredwell House
3. Cooper Union
4. McSorley's Ale House
5. St. Mark's-in-the-Bowery Church
6. Tomkins Square
7. Second Avenue Deli

East Village

Even the name **East Village** conjures up images of hippies, riots, drugs in the Alphabet blocks and all sorts of nefarious goings-on. Well, that all used to be true, and in small pockets may still be taking place, but this village has been transformed by artists, developers, shop-owners and restaurateurs. Try it, I think you'll like it. And just take the same amount of care you would during a walk in any other section of the city.

Start at the busy intersection of Fourth Ave., Lafayette and Astor Place, where you see Bernard Rosenthal's huge **black sculptured cube**. Across the street is the handsome Beaux Arts subway entrance.

Walk south on Lafayette St. On the west side is **Colonnade Row** (1833) with sweeping rows of Corinthian columns fronting four houses (originally nine), once homes for the **Astors** and **Vanderbilts**, as well as writers **Dickens, Thackeray** and **Washington Irving**.

On the east side of the street is **Joseph Papp's Public Theater**. ①
Its six theatres now reside in the building **John Jacob Astor** built in 1854 as the city's first free library. Take a minute to step in to see what is playing and perhaps to pick up tickets.

Continue to Fourth St., turn left to 29 E. Fourth St., and the Greek Revival **Old Merchant's House** (1830). **Seabury Tred-** ②
well and his family lived here in the 1800s and the house is still filled with the original interiors and furniture. Admission is by special arrangement. Call 777-1089.

Around the corner, walk north on Third Ave. about three blocks to **Cooper Union** on your left. A Saint-Gaudens statue of ③
founder **Peter Cooper** still sits in the garden. Cooper cooperated with **Cyrus Field** to develop the telegraph cable and with **Samuel F.B. Morse** to develop his telegraph.

Cooper Union, a tuition-free public college founded in 1895, has been an important part of this city's intellectual and liberal tradition. **Abraham Lincoln** spoke here; the **American Red Cross** and the **NAACP** began here and thousands of people were provided the kind of education Cooper himself was denied. In spite of his tremendous success, he was never able to read.

Turn right on Seventh St. The **Ukrainian Shop, Surma**, at #11 is filled with wonderful artifacts, painted eggs, embroidery, musical instruments and books. Across the street is **St. George's Ukrainian Catholic Church,** with a mosaic dome.

(4) At 15 Seventh St., you will come to **McSorley's Old Ale House** (1854). It also claims to be one of New York's oldest bars. In 1970, it finally permitted women on its premises. Take a minute to walk through and order a drink.

(5) Walk to Second Ave., then north to Tenth St. and **St. Mark's-in-the-Bowery Church** (1799). It was built on **Peter Styvesant's** estate and is the oldest continuously used church building in the city. It was restored following a fire in 1978. Walk around the church yard, now covered with cobblestones, to see where Peter and his relatives are buried.

Back down Second Ave. to Ninth St. Walk Ninth St. to
(6) **Tompkins Square**, about two blocks, and back on Eighth St. Since both the shops and restaurants change so rapidly in this area, I am not going to suggest specific places, but be assured there will be plenty of both. **St. Mark's Place** (Eighth St. in the East Village) was the center of the hip life of the beatniks in the 1950s and 60s.

Tompkins Square at your easternmost point on this walk has been the site for demonstrations since 1874 when the U.S.' first labor clash occurred. More recently in 1988 and 89, summer disturbances occurred when the city attempted to remove vagrants from the park and establish a curfew. But for the most part, things are now quiet around the park.

If you want a good lunch, just look around you. There are

dozens of good ethnic restaurants in the area. If you want a suggestion, when you walk Eighth St. back to Second Ave., turn right two blocks to the **Second Ave. Deli** (Second Ave. and ⑦ Tenth St.)

Notice the stars embedded in the sidewalk in front of the restaurant with the names of former Yiddish actors, a reminder of the many Yiddish theaters once located in this area. The deli even has its **Molly Picon** room, filled with memories of those days. No credit cards, please. Open daily from 7 a.m. to midnight.

As the East Village changes, more and more attractive shops and restaurants have opened.

If you choose to eat dinner in this area, you might well choose a charming French bistro, **Casanis**, located at 54 First St. between 1st and 2nd Aves. Telephone 777-1589. It only has 34 seats, so smoking is permitted. The tables are very close together, which encourages conversations with your neighbors, and they only take cash. Aside from these caveats, this may be one of your best French meals in the city. Look for the specials on the chalk board or check the menu for wonderful sweetbreads, rack of lamb or steak tartare. Prices are moderate.

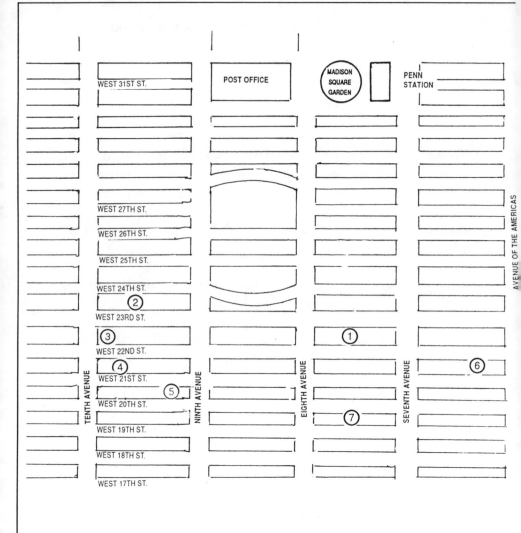

WEST 31ST ST.

POST OFFICE

MADISON SQUARE GARDEN

PENN STATION

WEST 27TH ST.

WEST 26TH ST.

WEST 25TH ST.

WEST 24TH ST.

② WEST 23RD ST.

③ WEST 22ND ST. ①

④ WEST 21ST ST. ⑥

⑤ WEST 20TH ST.

⑦ WEST 19TH ST.

WEST 18TH ST.

WEST 17TH ST.

TENTH AVENUE

NINTH AVENUE

EIGHTH AVENUE

SEVENTH AVENUE

AVENUE OF THE AMERICAS

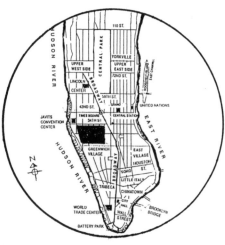

Chelsea

1. Chelsea Hotel
2. London Terrace Apartments
3. Empire Diner
4. General Theological Seminary
5. Cushman Row
6. Cemetery
7. The Billiard Club

Chelsea

This is one of the oldest and most mixed neighborhoods in New York. Tenements and shabby stores stand cheek by jowl with renovated town houses and trendy shops and restaurants. **Chelsea** runs from the Hudson River to Sixth Ave. and from 14th to 34th Sts., and takes its name from London's Chelsea Royal Hospital. The central part of New York's Chelsea was originally the country estate of **Clement Clark Moore's** family. Clergyman and classics scholar, Moore is best known for his 1822 poem, "A Visit from St. Nicholas."

During the 1880s, Chelsea was the center of a thriving theater district which later moved uptown while the artists who had lived here moved downtown to Greenwich Village.

Today's walk, which will take about one-half day, starts at the famous **Chelsea Hotel** on 23rd St., between Seventh and Eight ① Aves. The 12-story hotel was built in 1884. Cross the street so you can get a good look at the fabulous wrought iron balconies which stretch across the upper stories of the building. The lobby is an eclectic mix of kitsch and art, reflecting the variety of visitors who called the Chelsea home. Among them were **O. Henry, Sarah Bernhardt, Dylan Thomas, Brendan Behan, Arthur Miller**, and musicians **Virgil Thompson** and the **Sex Pistols**. If there is a center to Chelsea, it is in this building.

Walk west on 23rd. Between Ninth and Tenth Aves., you will see the great sweep of the 1930 **London Terrace Apartments**. ② Built during the depression, they have survived and flourished.

Turn the corner to your left at the corner of Tenth Avenue. A few steps will bring you to the famous **Empire Diner**, built in ③ 1976, but a reminder of the 1930's diners. Open 24 hours a day, it is a popular place for the "in crowd" at 3 or 4 in the morning. You can see limos standing outside its doors at that hour. You go here for the ambience, not the food.

Continue south on Tenth Ave., past the **Clement Clarke Moore Park,** between 22nd and 21st Aves. Turn left on 21st St. Here (4) you will find the **General Theological Seminary** (1883-1900) filling the entire block. During public hours, you can enter through the library building on Ninth Ave. For their Grand Design Tour, call 243-5150. Moore donated the land in 1830, requiring that the seminary remain on the site.

The **West Building,** 1853, is the oldest building in the complex and the oldest Gothic Revival building in New York City. At the **Chapel of the Good Shepherd,** note the great bronze doors and the 161-foot-square bell tower. **Hoffman Hall** at Tenth Ave. contains a mock medieval dining room and walk-in fireplaces. St. Mark's library is the new kid on this block.

(5) On the other side of the street, from 406-424, is the **Cushman Row** of Greek Revival houses, many of them in excellent condition. Particularly notice the fences with the cast-iron pineapples sitting atop the newel posts. These were once the homes of sea captains who used to place real pineapples on their doorsteps to announce their return and to let people know they could expect such exotic fare during their visits. This hospitality symbol later took this more permanent form.

At 404 W. 20th St. stands the oldest house (1829) in the district, with one clapboard side and a Greek Revival doorway.

Cross Ninth Ave. and you will be passing **St. Peter's Church.,** which sports a fence brought from downtown **Trinity Church**. It dates from 1790. The church is currently undergoing extensive remodeling.

Continue east on W. 20th St. to Sixth Ave. Turn left one block, (6) then left again on 21st St. Here you will find the **Third Cemetery** of the Spanish and Portuguese synagogue (1829-51). Note the magnificent ailanthus tree shading the stones.

Back to Sixth Ave., where you will see the 1875 cast-iron building, once the home of the **Hugh O'Neill Dry Good Store,** across the street. You are now in the center of what was once a fashionable shopping area called **Ladies' Mile**. And is again.

Sixth Ave. has again become a shopper's paradise. At the corner of 21st St. and 6th Ave. is a large **Barnes and Noble** book store with particularly good music, travel and children's sections and a very nice cafe on the second floor balcony.

Continue south to 19th St. and 6th Ave. to find **Bed Bath and Beyond** on one side of the street and **Today's Man** on the other. At 18th St. are **Old Navy** and **T J Max** stores.

For a break, at 17th St., you will find New York's **Foundling Hospital**, which celebrated its 125th anniversary in 1994. It was begun by two Sisters of Charity in 1869 with $5 and many prayers and is now a major institution serving children.

Around the corner on 16th St. is **St. Xavier's Catholic Church**. If it is open, walk up the steep steps to see the remarkable balconies and the Spanish interior.

At 15th St., turn east to visit a charming children's shop, **Kidding Around**, filled with toys, games, clothing and knowledgeable people who can help you find just the right things for your children or grandchildren.

There are not too many restaurants along Sixth Ave., but just walk over to Fifth Ave., where you will find the remarkable **Mesa Grill** and the more pedestrian **Au Bon Pan**.

If you want something a bit different, walk west on 19th St. to the **Billiard Club** at 220 W. 19th St., between Seventh and ⑦ Eighth Aves. This Victorian-looking billiard "hall" serves no alcohol, but does serve reasonably priced sandwiches and salads. You can also try your skill at billiards at one of their 33 tables.

Index

NOTES

NOTES

TRAVEL AHEAD?

London for the Independent Traveler. You can find more of the London you want with this marvelous self-guided tour book by Ruth Humleker. A travel classic. "It practically holds your hand with its step by step itineraries" says *Conde Nast's Traveler*. What more can we say? 38 maps, 236 pgs. **$12.95**

The Other Side of Sydney. Here's an independent traveler's guide to wonderful Australia's largest city, complete with information on the Olympics. Get the most out of Sydney without spending a fortune, find low-cost lodging, food, and harbor hot-spots. Complete with a special Sydneysider's pub tour. 21 maps, 236 pgs. **$15.95**

State by State Guide to Budget Motels. Find a good room for less money in both chain and independent motels throughout the U.S. Before you stay, check it out! Save the cost of this book your first night on the road. 416 pgs, 50 maps. **$12.95**

Going Abroad. A practical and humorous guide that tells how to use toilets throughout the world, including the formidable "squat" toilet. Gives special techniques and information on necessary stuff you may never have thought about, but should, if you are going abroad. Tells what to do when there's no toilet paper. A real bathroom survival guide (and a great gift book). 44 drawings, 144 pgs. **$12.95.**

Call to order your books today! Visa and Master Card orders accepted by telephone during business hours.

MARLOR PRESS, INC.

(612) 484-4600 or toll free **1-800-669-4908**

Photo: Pat Horner

Ruth Humleker lives in Manhattan. She is also the author of *London for the Independent Traveler*.